DAY-BY-DAY ITINERARIES FOR ONCE-IN-A-LIFETIME TWO-WHEEL ADVENTURES

Bicycle touring isn't just America's favorite sport. In cyclist-friendly Italy, it's become the hottest travel innovation on two wheels! And now you can get your own Italian adventure rolling by taking your healthy hobby abroad—and biking to all of the exciting destinations on Europe's sunniest peninsula. Great food, world-class wine, spectacular architecture and art—Italy has it all!

Tour the terraced villas of the Lake District. . . . Take a romantic six-day sojourn through Tuscany. . . . Discover Spoleto, Umbria's artistic heart. . . . Browse through Florence, not just a city but a living work of art. . . . Bike to the Leaning Tower of Pisa. . . . Delight in Lake Como, where charming harbor towns hug the hillsides. . . . Enjoy The Piedmont, a food and wine lover's paradise. . . . Get to—and relax at—Italy's greatest spas. It's all charted in this freewheeling course through the most beautiful bicycle-friendly country of all.

- A mile-by-mile guide to *all* of Italy's most exciting sights—even those off the beaten tourist path
- Maps, tips, money-saving strategies, and clearly marked routes for every level of cyclist
- Day-by-day itineraries for four complete week-long tours
- When to go, what to bring, where to stay
- Hotels and restaurants in every price range—and a glossary of bike-shop Italian.

GAY and KATHLYN HENDRICKS are psychologists who practice and teach in Colorado. They are also avid travelers who have toured all over the world on their bikes.

D0041134

GAY & KATHLYN HENDRICKS

BICYCLE TOURS

—— OF ——

ITALY

A PLUME BOOK

PLUME
Published by the Penguin Group
Penguin Books USA Inc., 375 Hudson Street,
New York, New York 10014, U.S.A.
Penguin Books Ltd, 27 Wrights Lane,
London W8 5TZ, England
Penguin Books Australia Ltd, Ringwood,
Victoria, Australia
Penguin Books Canada Ltd, 10 Alcorn Avenue,
Toronto, Ontario, Canada M4V 3B2
Penguin Books (N.Z.) Ltd, 182–190 Wairau Road,
Auckland 10, New Zealand

Penguin Books Ltd, Registered Offices:
Harmondsworth, Middlesex, England

First published by Plume,
an imprint of New American Library,
a division of Penguin Books USA Inc.

First Printing, May, 1992
1 3 5 7 9 10 8 6 4 2

 REGISTERED TRADEMARK—MARCA REGISTRADA

LIBRARY OF CONGRESS CATALOGING IN PUBLICATION DATA:
Hendricks, Gay.
    Bicycle tours of Italy / Gay and Kathlyn Hendricks.
    p. cm.
    ISBN 0-452-26803-6
    1. Bicycle touring—Italy—Guide-books. 2. Italy—Description and travel—
1975 —Guide-books. I. Hendricks, Kathlyn. II. Title.
GV1046.I8H46 1992
796.6'4'0945—dc20   91–38680
                                                                         CIP

Printed in the United States of America
Set in Times Roman

Designed by Steven N. Stathakis

WARNING!

Bicycling is a strenuous sport. Before embarking on these tours, it is advisable to check with your physician to make sure you are in sound enough health to cope with the rigors of several hours of physically demanding exercise a day.

CONTENTS

GENERAL HINTS, TIPS, AND STRATEGIES FOR BICYCLE TOURING   29

PART TWO: THE TOURS

NOTE

The authors have accepted no complimentary rooms, meals, or gifts throughout any of the tours described in this book. Similarly, we have not traveled with or on any gift equipment of any kind. Therefore, you can be assured that our recommendations are based solely on personal opinion. Likewise, any opinions we express are solely our responsibility.

INTRODUCTION: WHY GO BICYCLE TOURING IN ITALY?

I was not yet sixteen when I understood a great deal, from having ridden bicycles for so long, about style, speed, grace, purpose, value, form, integrity, health, humor, music, breathing, and finally and perhaps best of all, the relationship between the beginning and the end.
—WILLIAM SAROYAN, from *The Bicycle Rider in Beverly Hills*

WE MUST CONFESS HERE AT THE OUTSET THAT ITALY IS our favorite place to go bicycle touring. Some of you have seen our other two books on cycling in France and the British Isles. Both of those areas have given us many years of satisfying exploration. But Italy is special for a number of reasons. The first is the Italian people. You will not find many "Italians" in Italy. Italy has not been a unified country for very long—only about a hundred years—and very few Italians think of themselves as such. There is a strong regional identification, and this quality lends a special flavor to each area we have toured.

But back to the people. Here you will find a genuine

warmth and caring for others that will be visible to you in your simple interactions with people. Sit in a village square some Sunday afternoon and watch how warmly the Italians treat their children. The kids sparkle, and their parents sparkle with pride. Also dear to a cyclist's heart is the Italian generosity when it comes to helping travelers. Many times we have stopped for directions only to have the person insist on leading us to the hotel or attraction we were seeking. And if you don't speak Italian (ours is primitive at best) the constant use of body language makes communication easy.

In our visits over the past decade we have noticed a clear difference between big-city Italy and the rest of the country. Cities such as Genoa, Naples, and particularly Rome are frantic, smoggy, and outrageously expensive. The people in the cities seem markedly less friendly than in the countryside, though the same could certainly be said for France, England, and the U.S. Only a suicidal cyclist would venture to ride in Rome—even walking there can be hazardous to your health. For this reason, the tours we describe for you in this book steer you away from the big cities, except for Florence. Florence is a happy exception as cities go, having retained many of its small-town traditions as it has grown.

Outside the cities, you will find yourself greatly respected as a cyclist. Bicycles are sacred in Italy; cyclists own the back roads. In other words, cyclists in the Italian countryside expect the right-of-way, and they get it. Many times we have labored up a long hill, followed respectfully by a line of cars who could not pass. This does not mean that you can be careless, but it certainly is a pleasant feeling to be so well regarded.

The scenery in the tours we have mapped out is stupendous. There is really nothing like it in any of the places we have been in the world. Each of the tours we have selected gives the cyclist a different Italy. From the grandeur of the Lake District to the quiet nobility of the Piedmont Wine Country, from the rolling hills of Tuscany to the medieval spires of Umbria, there is something for everyone in Italy. You will notice that the tours we describe all take place in the northern and central portions of Italy. The South is a different story. It is wilder, rougher, and more challenging in many ways. While it is possible to have fun touring the South, we have chosen not to recommend this region for several reasons. First, the heat during the main cycling season can be awesome. It is not uncommon to have temperatures well over 100° Fahrenheit, with friends of ours reporting 120° on one of their tours. Personally, we have a hard time riding when it's up near 100°, and anything higher is downright dangerous. A second reason we have not advocated any southern Italian tours is crime. Practically everybody we have ever talked to who has toured southern Italy has had something stolen. If you are in southern cities such as Naples, Palermo, and Brindisi, it is best to keep your eye on your belongings at all times. Make sure bicycles are well secured and indoors at night. Perhaps the problem will decrease in the future, but in the meantime we have found cycling to be safer, easier, and more fun in the northern and central regions.

Now, back to the wonders of Italy. Not long ago we stood on a hill outside Florence and remarked that here was an entire city that was itself a masterpiece. There was nothing—not a skyscraper, not a radar tower—to mar the sweep of the eye across the vista, made luminous by the soft afternoon light. Of course, Italy is also the repository of many of the world's greatest art treasures. Even if you have a low tolerance for museums and cathedrals, we predict you will be deeply moved by a trip through the Uffizi in Florence and Saint Peter's in Rome.

Italy has been inhabited at least as far back as the Bronze Age. Prominent among the early residents of this land were the Etruscans, a mysterious group of people whose language hasn't been decoded to this day. Many museums feature artifacts of the Etruscans, who were in evidence several hundred years before Rome began to be constructed about 800 B.C. Latins began to congregate around Rome to escape the powerful Etruscans. The Latins resisted subjugation until about 600 B.C., but then fell sway to the warlike Etruscans. In some areas of Italy one can see several layers of its history built on top of each other. There is the ancient Etruscan contribution, followed by the Roman Empire's magnificent additions. Then, superimposed on the Roman antiquities will be the results of the Renaissance, and often a modern layer. In Rome, for example, we have marveled to turn a corner and find an ancient ruin sandwiched between a Renaissance building and a modern structure. There are very few places in the world where this juxtaposition of cultures and historical eras can be seen.

ITALIAN FOOD

Italy has one of the world's greatest cuisines, and it is ideal for the needs of the cyclist. Most people, having grown up thinking of Italian food as spaghetti with red sauce, are amazed by the variety of options available in Italy.

Italy's strong regional identities make for a great variety of dining experiences. Around Rome, for example, you may have a fish soup, a pasta dish made with *cannelloni*, and end up with a *zabaglione*, that rich eggy, frothy dessert every good restaurant will feature. Up near Venice, though, you may well see the locals eating liver and onions, which almost no one associates with Italian cuisine. In the Lake District there will almost always be *ossobuco* on the menu, a veal shank simmered slowly until wonderfully tender, then served over rice. The farther north you go the more likely you will be to find *risotto* on the menu. Using a distinctive round-grained rice, the northern Italians then add butter, spices, and other complements.

We will have more to say about the flavors of Italy in the introductions to the specific tours.

THE WINES AND LIQUORS OF ITALY

We are not big drinkers, so we cannot give you much personal information on this subject. Sometimes we have a glass of wine with dinner, and almost always ask the serving person for a recommendation. So far we have not been disappointed in any way. Italy is one of those rare places where it is hard to get a bad meal or a bad glass of wine.

The people of Italy have been producing fine wines for a long time. The Etruscans knew how to ferment grapes, and since then the Italians have perfected the art. Now more of the countryside is under cultivation for wine than for food.

One drink that we always see throughout Italy is Campari. A beautiful red color, this bitter potion, served over ice with soda water, is a popular drink with the sidewalk café crowd. Also popular are the various liqueurs, including Strega and Galliano, both herb-flavored, and Sambucca, a licorice-flavored drink served for some odd reason with a coffee bean floating in it. We also see many locals drinking Cinzano, a vermouth that they flavor with lemon and soda.

No matter what your interests—scenic vistas, art, food, wine—you will likely find Italy rich in possibilities. Beyond all the attractions, though, is the feel of Italy. The warmth of the people, the smiles of the children, the glorious light of late afternoon—all these elements and more combine to make Italy an almost intoxicating experience. Add to it the simple pleasures of the cycling life and you have a recipe for an ideal vacation.

PART ONE

MAKING YOUR TOUR A SUCCESS

GENERAL

INFORMATION

ON BICYCLE TOURING

IN ITALY

WHAT KIND OF TOUR SHOULD YOU TAKE?

There is only one choice you need to make to get started: whether to go solo or to take an organized tour. Your choice will determine other factors, such as whether you will be renting a bike or taking your own. Both ways have advantages and disadvantages. For a first-timer it is easiest to join an organized tour. This is how the authors did it the first time (in France), and looking back on it we are grateful to have done so. However, we did not have the book you are holding in your hand, which was written specifically to give the first-time or experienced cyclist the know-how to go solo from the start.

Let's look at some advantages and disadvantages of the solo and organized-tour approaches. The great advantage of an organized tour is that someone else handles the logistical details. Join a tour and you will be handed a marked map in the morning, and the key to your room at night. Your restaurants are chosen for you, the best little roads are pointed out, and your bike is kept in good working order. Above all, a sagwagon follows with your luggage and, should you need it, can carry you. First-time travelers can get frustrated having to contend with all these details when they are already bicycling several hours more a day than they are likely used to.

Another advantage of an organized tour is that you have a ready-made social group. There will usually be no shortage of dinner-table companions or fellow wine connoisseurs with whom to visit the local vineyards. You could, of course, be stuck with a bunch of people you turn out not to like. Usually there is plenty of space, even on an organized tour, to spread out and do your own thing, but the evenings will often be spent in marathon dining experiences. If you do not like your companions, the nights can be long.

For many, the cost is a major consideration of an organized tour. Plan on spending around $200 per person per day. Our first tour was an eight-day affair which cost $1695. For both of us, then, the cost was about $3400 for an eight-day trip. Of course, this price did not include airfare or a few days in Paris on either end. Let's take a closer look at the numbers. If you travel as a twosome, you are consuming one night's lodging, two continental breakfasts and two dinners. Lunch will almost always be on your own, although most tours feature a picnic or two at the company's expense. On our first organized tour, we noted the cost of the rooms, which were always displayed on the door. Seldom were they over the equivalent of $50. Seldom were the dinners more than $50 per person. If your wine consumption is measured more in bottles than glasses, plan on spending somewhat more. So, even if you throw in $10 apiece for croissants and coffee, there is still $200–250 a day that is going toward the profits of the touring company. This is the premium you pay for maps, the sagwagon, and a guide. We are certainly not saying this profit margin is inappropriate or high; in fact, we think it is a pretty good deal. The question is whether you could find something better to do with your money.

The first time out, you may find that it's worth it to pay

the premium. But on future trips we bet you will go solo. Going solo, or with a few close friends, has tremendous advantages. You are free to make your own choices. With a little advance planning, a good map, and the *Guide Michelin*, you can run your own trip. With that extra $200 a day in your pocket, go wild with a couple of dinners at a three-star restaurant. We guarantee that you will never forget the experience of dining at a restaurant that people wait a year to get reservations for. A friend of ours dined at a three-star restaurant in Italy where the bill for four people came to $1200. Sounds high, but he's still talking about it.

Let's look into some of the details of going solo. One word that sums up the difference is *weight*. You will have to carry about ten pounds of your clothing, toiletries, and other essentials in your panniers. Ten extra pounds makes your bike harder to pedal and makes it handle a little differently. Neither of these considerations is earthshaking, in our experience, but you should build them into your plans. Put ten pounds extra on your bike when you are getting in shape for the trip; it is not wise to wait until you get there to find out how a loaded bike handles. If you decide you want to camp out throughout your tour, it would be safe to double the weight estimate to twenty or more pounds. Neither of us enjoys camping, so you will have to look for another book—there are several—to explain the joys of European camping.

Another attractive option is to take your own bikes and rent a car to haul them from place to place. Renting a car in Italy is no problem, but it is expensive. Plan on double what you might pay in the U.S. The last time we rented a car in Italy, the tab was $1100 for two weeks. (With gas going for $4–5 a gallon, you will appreciate the tiny cars they drive over there.) Nevertheless, renting a car makes life easier and certainly more mobile. You won't be at the mercy of the train schedule in the least, and you can easily get to many places you might skip without a car. On one of our recent tours we rented a car and based in one town in each area we wanted to tour. We did day loops, returning to home base at night, then we drove the car to a new area and rode from there each day.

This book is written with the adventurous but comfort-loving bicycle tourer in mind. You travel light, you stay at inns, and you only carry a modest amount of weight on your bike. The last thing we want to do when we finish six hours of riding is to pitch a tent and wait for the water to boil. We want a hot bath waiting and a good cup of coffee or tea at the ready.

After trying many different ways, our unhesitating recommendation is to go solo or with close friends, take your own bikes, tour specific regions (such as the four great trips described later), and get from region to region by train. An evening or two of advance planning, all of which you do with the information in the book, will yield assurance that you will always have a bed waiting for you at the end of the day.

WHAT KIND OF BIKE IS BEST? HOW DO YOU GET IT THERE?

Having tried several different ways, the authors have developed a strong opinion on this subject. *Take your own bike, preferably a mountain bike.* Here's why: Renting a bicycle sounds like a good idea, but in fact it is usually a disaster. Once, for example, we attempted to rent bikes in a large Scottish city. According to the travel guide we were using, there were oodles of bike shops, each bursting with rental bikes. After going to three bike shops we found one that rented bikes and were shown to a dim room. The owner invited us to pick out the ones we wanted. After a half hour of searching we found two that needed only minor repairs. We told the owner the repairs that were needed, and he nodded gravely, returning in a few minutes with a pair of pliers and a couple of terminally greasy wrenches. He handed these to us and left for the day, telling us to stuff the tools under the doormat when we were finished. On another occasion, we wanted to rent bikes in Chengdu, China, a city of several million people and at least a million bikes. We were shown to an underground garage with bicycles as far as the eye could see. But we had to sort through over thirty bikes to find ones on which the brakes worked. Enough said.

Italy is not blessed with many places to rent bikes, anyway. There are some shops in the major cities, but it would be a mistake to count on having a good experience on a rented bike. This leaves the option of buying a bike there or bringing your own. If you don't mind a few days of waiting time after you arrive, buying and outfitting a bicycle in Italy is not a bad idea. Mountain bikes are catching on there and will probably become more widely available over the next few years. If you expect a bargain, though, forget it. Bicycles are generally expensive in Europe and particularly so in Italy.

TAKING YOUR OWN BIKE

Taking your own bike is not as hard as it sounds, and you will know what you are getting. We recommend mountain bikes. Yes, they are a little heavier than touring bikes, but they have the advantage of a more comfortable ride. Many of the choice roads you will want to ride can be rough. And many European towns, even larger ones, are at least partly paved with cobblestones. These are pretty to look at, but brain-rattlingly difficult on a thin-tired bike. With your fat-tired mountain bike, you will bump pleasantly over cobblestones and charge down primitive country lanes. Dirt roads will even be an option; not so on a thin-tired bike. If you keep your mountain bike tires properly inflated, flats will be very rare. Also not so on a thin-tired bike, where, by our rough count over the years, we averaged about one flat a week. Since switching to mountain bikes some years ago, we have had only three flats all told. In fact, on our roughest trip of all time, a two-week journey through Tibet, we never had a single flat. If you already have a sturdy touring bike by all means take it. But if you are just getting started, at least consider mountain bikes as your touring companions.

Airline regulations vary in regard to how you take your bike, and how much they charge. Many airlines take bikes free, but you need to check in advance so you won't be surprised. Some airlines do not make you pack your bike in a box, while others are adamant on the subject. Putting a bike in a box is not difficult, but requires a visit to a bike shop to pick up the carton. It also requires a few minutes of work with simple tools. You need to remove the pedals, turn the handlebars sideways, and usually remove at least the front wheel. The airport is not the place to perform this operation for the first time. With mountain bikes, turning the handlebars may be more difficult, requiring a loosening of the brake cables. A few minutes at a bike shop is usually sufficient to learn how to do this on your particular bike.

Here is a suggestion: Show up at the airport, with bike and the tools you will need. Bring a carton, but leave it over in the corner. See if the airline will take your bike without putting it in a box. Sometimes they will and sometimes they won't. Sometimes they will give you the same heavy plastic used to wrap skis. This is better than a box, in our opinion, because putting the bike out of sight in a box increases your chances of damage. The baggage handlers are more likely to be rough with a bike they cannot see than one they can. In our experience, the most dangerous part of your bike's journey is while it is in the hands of the airline. This argues again in favor of taking mountain bikes. They are much more rugged than their lighter cousins and thus can withstand more of a beating at the hands of the airlines. Regardless, you need to be prepared to do some adjusting and even repairing when you arrive at your destination. On a couple of occasions, we have had to make a trip to a local bicycle shop on first arriving, due to some damage done to a bike on the flight over. It takes a little time, but we have yet to be in a country where there was not some local genius with a wrench who could do the repair.

BUYING A BIKE IN EUROPE

Another option is to buy a bicycle when you get to Europe. Many people think they can get a good bargain by buying their bike in Europe. Forget it. This may have been true at one time, but no longer. Some people may think they can get a higher quality machine in Europe than they can in the U.S.

Again, forget it. With a couple of rare and expensive exceptions, you will find better quality in a good American or Japanese bike than you will in a European model. The authors ride Klein, Trek, and Stumpjumper machines, and we have yet to see anything in Europe we would trade them for.

USING TRAINS ON YOUR BIKE TOUR

Bikes and trains are a perfect combination. We find trains to be both exciting and restful ways to travel. In Europe, they are more highly developed than anywhere else we have toured. All trains will let you take your bike, though the exact procedure has some variations. Europeans, particularly the French and the Italians, are very respectful of bikes. Your bike will be well treated; theft is rare, though of course you need to bring a chain and lock.

In England you can often ride your bike down the track to the baggage car and load it yourself. There is no fee. When the train gets where it is going, you unlock it and ride away down the platform. As you might expect if you've traveled in Europe before, France, Italy, and Spain have rendered this commonsense and workable procedure into something more complex. First, there is a charge, usually the equivalent of a few dollars. Second, your bike may in certain circumstances go on a different train than you, especially if you are going on an express train. Don't worry, we haven't heard of any cases where the bikes disappeared into thin air. But sometimes there can be a delay of a few hours or even a day until your bike arrives. The rail company guarantees that it will arrive in seventy-two hours. Usually the station will hold it free for a day, but if you leave it longer you can expect a charge. The northern countries, such as Germany and Holland, each have their own particular twists on the regulations. The best thing to do is to buy your ticket, then find out what the rules are for the train on which you are booked. It rarely takes more than a few extra minutes to do your bicycle business. Bikes are such an integral part of life in Europe that the policies are well worked out, even though they vary slightly from place to place. If you encounter an obstacle, such as a particularly difficult train official who tells you that under no circumstances can you take your bike to wherever you are going, persist. Go higher up. A way can usually be found. Once we stood in line behind an English biker who wanted to go from Tours to Nice, in the south of France. "Utterly impossible," said the clerk, who was not having a good day. "Bikes not allowed on this train." Much argument ensued. Loud voices, waving arms, slurs on the patrimony of each. Finally the clerk went on break, and was replaced by another fellow. "Absolutely. No problem, monsieur." Within minutes, the Englishman was on his way to Nice, bike and all.

Here, is the general procedure to follow. First, buy your ticket to your destination. With ticket in hand, go to the baggage counter and choose the train. Try to find one that takes accompanying baggage (since this will allow you to go on the same train as your bike). Being on the same train as our bikes always makes us feel more comfortable, although we have never lost one. Next, register your bike by filling out a form, and hand over your bike (you should get a receipt). Remove all the easily stolen items like pump, water bottle, and handlebar packs. Some railway stations also have a cardboard envelope which fits around your bike.

Get on the train, and when you reach your destination, pick up your bike by handing over your receipt. Sometimes your bike will not arrive when you do, and you will need to come back a couple of times to find it. If you are picking up your bike at an out-of-the-way station, don't be surprised if there's nobody there during the afternoon siesta time.

Does all this sound complicated? It's not, really, and after a few times it will make perfect sense. At larger Italian railway stations you can pick up a booklet that gives you up-to-date information on the procedures, which change from time to time. Also, a booklet is available at large stations which provides the layout and services of all the major Italian train terminals.

MAPS

Although you could probably get by with the daily route maps we have provided in this book, it would be wiser to buy a good map of the region to supplement our maps. We always buy the Michelin map of the area we plan to tour. Michelin maps are the best we have found, except for the Bartholomew maps of England. If possible, buy them before you leave the U.S. They are always more expensive in Italy than they are in North America. If you cannot locate a good map source nearby, write the Michelin people for their catalogue: Michelin, P.O. Box 5022, New Hyde Park, NY 11042.

WHEN TO GO: WEATHER, FELLOW TRAVELERS, AND SUCH

You may be wondering what happens if it rains during your tour. The answer: You stay inside that day, or get wet. In our experience, it doesn't happen that often. We can only remember a few days of being absolutely stopped by the weather. Part of the trick is good clothing; another part of it is good planning. A lot of it is good luck.

Gore-Tex is a great friend to the bicycle tourer. We have Gore-Tex jackets in two weights, along with riding pants made out of the same material. These items have proved worth their weight in gold on many trips. We have both owned rain capes, but have given them up in favor of the Gore-Tex jacket-pants combination. Capes are voluminous and are always getting tangled up in things. In many instances, your rain cape will act as a portable steam bath, and you will ride both wet and hot. Gore-Tex is expensive, but will make up for it in convenience and long-term use. The material is also useful in dealing with wind, which is an even bigger challenge than rain.

Wind can be heartbreaking as well as making your heart pound. On a recent tour we climbed 10 miles steadily uphill to a mountain pass, dreaming of the ride down from the top.

Alas, when we got to the top we found a headwind blowing at gale force. We rode downhill in *first* gear, straining all the way against the wind at about 1 mile an hour. It was psychologically discouraging as well as physically exhausting. On the flip side, we have been the recipients of some inspiring tailwinds. There is nothing like the exhilaration of flying down the road at 25 miles an hour with only the barest effort.

Rain and wind can be obstacles at times, but neither needs to be monitored like heat. Unless you plan ahead and drink in advance, you can get in serious trouble by dehydrating yourself. By the time you get thirsty you may have already passed the critical point. We have seen many a cyclist with a flushed face, a headache, and a pair of quivering legs—all from ignoring the body's need for water. You have to plan ahead. Begin with a few extra glasses of water in the morning, and keep drinking as you go along, even if you are not thirsty. If you don't trust the local water, you will find noncarbonated bottled water everywhere.

There are some places and times of the year when it is not wise to ride in the middle of the day. As the summer goes on, the heat in Italy can get brutal. But the hot snap can happen anywhere, and you will simply have to monitor the weather. Get on the road early, and take a siesta from noon to five or so. The depleted feeling you can get from too much sun and heat can be especially enervating on a bike, as the wind on your body will often make you feel cooler than you are.

Italy is hot throughout the cycling season—May to October—except for the cooler northern areas of the Lake District and Piedmont. The humidity is generally low, though, so 90° in Tuscany does not feel like 90° in New Jersey. All big-city Italians who can do so flee the cities on the weekends in July and particularly August. They will want to stay at the same inns and eat at the same restaurants you do. The authors happen to be allergic to crowds, so for us, May and September are perfect months to travel. Service is better, the roads are quieter, and the weather can often be wonderful. If you want to go to Italy in July and August, it is imperative that you make plenty of advance reservations.

There is no way to predict what kind of weather you are going to get. Our suggestion: Just go. Pick a time when you can do it and do it. Do your planning but don't worry about the weather. Chances are you will not be inconvenienced by the weather more than a couple of times. If you are, there are worse things in life than a stroll around an Italian town on a rainy afternoon or a long day under the covers.

ITALIAN CURRENCY

The first time we went to Italy the exchange rate was very easy to keep in mind: $1 U.S. was equal to just about 1,000 lira. Since then the lira has slipped somewhat. On our last tour (1991) the exchange rate was $1 to about 1,200 lira. In other words, 1,000 lira was worth about 80 cents. On that trip we stopped in at the local Ferrari dealership in Milan and priced one. The windshield was barely large enough to contain all the zeros: 240,000,000 lira. One Italian told us, "We like to have a lot of money even though it's not worth anything."

The money may confuse you for a couple of days, but it becomes easy to decipher with practice. In addition, the gracious Italians are always ready to help you make change. One never sees the surly attitude that can be a nuisance in France.

WHAT TO TAKE AND WHAT NOT TO TAKE: CLOTHING AND OTHER NECESSITIES OF THE ROAD

The most practical and efficient way to pack is to take no more than your panniers can carry. If you get a good pair of panniers, they will serve as your carry-on luggage on the airplane. Pannier technology is changing rapidly, and whatever advice we give you might be obsolete by the time you read this. Visit a good bike shop, and tell them what you are looking for: high-quality panniers that attach and detach easily, have plenty of room, and are easy to pack and repack. They should be as waterproof as you can afford and made of a material that is easy to clean.

Here is what we took on a recent tour. It is a fairly good representation of what is needed on a one-week tour. On this particular tour we were going to be dining at several very fancy restaurants, so we needed clothing that would not make us look out of place.

Riding Clothes and Equipment

helmet
gloves
Gore-Tex jacket and pants
2 pairs of riding shorts (with reinforced seats)
3 cotton T-shirts
3 pairs of socks
1 pair of silk thermal underwear
1 pair of running shoes (special bike touring shoes are available which are also comfortable enough for walking, but we have found that good running shoes work just as well)

Casual and Fancy Wear

1 pair of jeans
1 pair of casual slacks
1 light wool sweater
1 pair of dress shoes
underwear
(for Kathlyn) Two silk evening outfits—slacks, top, and matching jacket
2 pairs of dress socks/stockings
(for Gay) 1 indestructible wool sport coat
2 shirts
1 tie

Miscellaneous

toiletries, carefully chosen and packed in a small kit: take a roll of
    your favorite brand of toilet paper, as the Italians have quaint
    ideas on this subject.
small first aid kit, including Band-Aids, antiseptic cream, aspirin,
    tweezers, scissors, moleskin
bathing suits
sunglasses
sunscreen and lip cream (absolutely essential)
2 well-chosen thick paperback books
camera
maps
tool kit, chain lubricant, 2 spare tubes (your water bottle and pump
    fit on your bike, so we are not counting those)

Total weight apiece: slightly under 10 pounds

You may want to invest in a handlebar pack or "fanny"
pack. It is nice to be able to get easily at frequently used
items (like map, lip cream, and camera) without opening your
panniers. If you buy the kind that straps around your waist
you can also use it as a day-pack when you are on foot.

WHAT AND HOW TO EAT

Food and athletic performance is a subject of much contro-
versy. To steer clear of this tempest in a stewpot, we will
simply tell you how we have found it best to eat on a tour.
You can try out our approach; feel free to modify it or change
it altogether to suit your particular metabolism.

First, we do not like to load up with a big breakfast in
the morning. Coffee and a couple of rolls are perfect. As it
happens, this traditional Italian breakfast is available everywhere, though sometimes it is transformed into bread, butter,
and jelly. Complex carbohydrates are good energy food and sit
lightly in the stomach. This latter consideration is an important one for the authors, who do not like to pedal with a full

sensation in the belly. We prefer to breakfast lightly, and then to eat frequent, light snacks as the day proceeds. If we are going to have a big protein-rich meal, we do it at night, after the main exercise of the day is over.

Finding great cycling food is not difficult in Italy—resisting it is difficult. Even a town of modest size will have a wonderful bakery, full of luscious tarts, cakes, and cookies. For this reason, we urge you not to bring your diet consciousness to Italy with you. Even if you've been a macrocosmic vegetarian for years, try something different for a change. You may not want to eat their way for the rest of your life, but enjoy it for a week or two. Besides, considerable research has been done on the health benefits of the Mediterranean diet. It seems that olive oil, vegetables, fruit and pasta—the heart of the Mediterranean approach to eating—are also good for the human heart.

For those of you who are weight conscious, bike touring is a blessing. It is hard to gain much weight while you are pedaling five or six hours a day. Biking burns up 300–600 calories an hour (compared to approximately 80 calories an hour watching TV), so you can eat with impunity. On one trip we each lost about five pounds, while on another we gained two or three. It is interesting that even on a cross-country bike trip of a couple of months, you will likely not gain or lose much weight. You will probably look leaner because of more muscle tissue, but everyone we have ever talked to about their long-distance journey said they stayed about the same weight.

One thing that has always surprised us about Italy is the lack of great salads. One of the mainstays of our diet at home is a big bowl of imaginative greenery. Not so the Italians. They put a lot of their attention into antipasto dishes—marinated vegetables, seafood bits, cold pasta salads—but the big green salad is something of a rarity. The antipasti are great, though, and easily make up for the absence of salad once you get used to them.

Excellent restaurants are everywhere. If a place calls itself a *ristorante*, it usually has a full menu. You may be expected to order several courses. If the place calls itself a *trattoria* or a *pizzeria*, you can get lighter fare, and it will be perfectly acceptable to order one thing, like a pizza. If it is called a bar, you can, of course, get drinks, but don't expect any hot food. Usually cold sandwiches are available in bars, unless they make a point of advertising that they have hot food.

One of our most pleasing discoveries was that price does not always mean quality. There are incredibly expensive and famous dining establishments that are simply tourist traps. But the true glory of traveling is to discover the unheralded country inn or neighborhood restaurant that serves a transcendent soup or an unforgettable dessert. These are the special moments you will always remember, because they will be free of pomp, circumstance, and hype. You will simply be treated to the cooking of people who adore food and who have their hearts and not simply their pocketbooks in it. Our best meals in Europe have always been at out-of-the-way, nonfamous restaurants.

If you are inclined to the conservative in matters of food, here is your chance to stretch. Order a dish on the menu that you cannot translate—be surprised at what you get. What, you may exclaim, if I get snails or some sort of obscure organ? Eat it! You may be pleased to discover you like what you get.

WATER

Bottled water is available everywhere. The tap water in Italy is all right and probably safe to drink, but we tend to order bottled water. In fact, we fancy ourselves gourmets of bottled water. If you want noncarbonated water in Italy, be sure to specify by saying *"no gas"* or *"senza gas."* If you want bubbles, say *"frizzante."* Far and away the top water in all of Europe, in our opinion, is Volvic, bottled in France. It has a vibrant, energetic taste without any mineral overtones. We even go out of our way to find it here in the U.S. In Italy it is a little hard to find, except in the northern parts close to France. Italy has dozens of waters of its own, some of which are close to being in Volvic's league. The best Italian water we found is called Norda, and is available all over Northern Italy. A close runner-up is Vera, with San Bernardino also being of good quality.

CUSTOMS

Most of the things you are likely to bring into Italy will be duty-free. At this writing, the customs quotas on common items are two cameras, ten rolls of film, one video camera or movie camera with ten tapes or rolls of film, two cartons of cigarettes, two bottles of opened liquor. On the way back to the U.S., you can bring $400 worth of goods duty-free. Keep your receipts in case you get questioned coming back in.

TELEPHONES

Phone calls from Italy back to North America have become much easier and more reliable over the past few years. Now you can dial direct. The procedure works like this: Dial 001, then dial the number in the U.S. or Canada. For example, you would dial 001-415-777-7777 to get a number in San Francisco. If you want to charge the call to your credit card, dial 170 and (if things are going your way) you will get someone who speaks English.

We have had mixed results with local calls and calls from one region of Italy to another. Persistence pays off: eventually, we have always gotten through.

GETTING LAUNDRY DONE

Almost all hotels and inns will see to it that your laundry is done, and done well, but it tends to be two or three times the price you might pay if you do it yourself. Do-it-yourself laundromats are also quite expensive, but substantially less than hotels. Laundries that do it for you will often charge less than the hotel, but make sure you pin them down on how long it is going to take. Some friends of ours had to delay their departure by several days once because of a communication breakdown about when their clothes would be done. If you are having your Gore-Tex articles done by a laundry, make sure they wash it and do not dry-clean it.

CLOSINGS AND HOLIDAYS

Most of Italy comes to a grinding halt during the siesta hours, from noon or so until anywhere from 3:00 to 4:30 P.M. Sometimes we have found this custom to be a real problem. Forgetting to pack any food in the morning, we have arrived in a small town at lunchtime only to find the only grocery store locked up tight. In larger towns there will always be a bar or restaurant open, though, and the cities will be full of thriving restaurants. Many restaurants close on Sunday evening, and many others close on Monday too. To protect yourself, call first, because some restaurants have peculiar closings such as for Wednesday lunch or Tuesday dinner.

Everything will be closed on the following holidays: January 1, Easter Sunday and Monday, April 25 (Liberation Day), May 1 (Labor Day), August 15 (Assumption Day), November 1 (All Saints' Day), December 8 (Feast of the Immaculate Conception), and December 25 and 26.

ITALIAN ROADS AND ROAD SIGNS

In France, England, and several other European countries, even the tiniest back road is carefully numbered on road signs. In Italy, by contrast, there are almost never any numbers on the smaller roads. The maps will have numbers on the roads; it's just the roads that don't have any numbers on them. After the initial shock wore off we got used to it. It can be frustrating at first, though.

There are several road signs that are handy to have a translation for. One that you will see a lot in Italy says "Senso Unico," and it means "one way." In the center of many towns there will be a Senso Unico route through town, as well as a two-way route. For cyclists, the one-way route can be a less frantic way to get through the heart of the city. Another handy sign is the one to watch for as you enter town: "Centro." This sign is guiding you toward the center of town. Many Italian roads, especially as you near larger towns, have roundabouts. Often you will have to proceed through several roundabouts to get to the center of town. Just keep following the Centro sign and you'll get there. The Italian word for "exit" is *uscita*; their word for a customs check point is *dogana*. On our Lake District Tour you will pass in and out of Switzerland a couple of times and will need to stop for customs checks. We usually have been waved right through, though, except for a couple of occasions when our little electronic typewriter excited their interest.

ELECTRICAL DEVICES

The prongs on the plugs in Italy are round, so you will need some kind of adapter to use any North American gadgets you bring. Perhaps with Europe moving toward greater unification they will reach agreement on what kind of plugs to use. In the meantime, you will also probably need a transformer, as Italy runs mostly on 220. Get the equipment you need before you go, if possible. Otherwise be prepared to pay much steeper prices at Italian appliance shops.

EMERGENCIES

The Italian emergency number that corresponds to the U.S. 911 is 113. Calling this number will bring a police officer or an ambulance, and, though we have never had to use it, we have heard that the service is prompt. Should you have health problems or need an English-speaking person to help you, the U.S. embassy in Rome can be reached at 06-46-741. Canadians in need of help may call their embassy at 06-440-3028.

MAIL

You can get mail at Italian post offices by having your correspondents add the words *fermo posta* after your name and the post office. They will hold it for you until you flash your passport at them. Stamps are available for outgoing mail at tobacco shops and sometimes at shops that sell postcards. Mail service in Italy is the source of many jokes among the locals.

HANDY ITALIAN WORDS FOR COMMUNICATING WITH BICYCLE SHOPS

Bicycle shops are everywhere in Italy, but many of their employees do not speak English. Here are some technical words that, when supplemented with sign language, may help you get your needs met.

English	Italian
brake	freno
cable	cavo
chain	catena
crank	manovella
derailleur	cambio
fork	forcella
freewheel	ruota libera
handlebar	manubrio
hub	mozzo
lock	lucchetto
pedal	pedale
pump	pompa
rim	cerchione
saddle	sella
spoke	raggio

English	Italian
tire	pneumatico
valve	valvola
wheel	ruota

GENERAL HINTS, TIPS, AND STRATEGIES FOR BICYCLE TOURING

IN THIS CHAPTER WE WILL COVER A NUMBER OF THOSE aspects of bike touring that you might otherwise have to learn the hard way. In fact, that's the way we learned many of the following skills, by making a lot of mistakes. Perhaps you will be able to save yourself time, energy, and sore anatomy by trying out some of this hard-won knowledge.

SAFETY

The most important part of any tour is staying healthy and intact. Europe is probably the safest populated place on earth to ride your bike, but you will still need to keep an eye out for your well-being all the time. Italians are legendary when it comes to wild driving. Italians on motorcycles are even wilder than in cars. Weekends are when the motorcyclists take to the road, releasing all that pent-up energy from the work week, and venting their hormones.

Although Italians are more respectful of cyclists, the sheer numbers with which they take to the roads make them a factor to be reckoned with, especially on weekends. Where possible, stay off the heavily trafficked roads. Except for a few hard-to-avoid places, all our tours steer you toward small roads and their even smaller country cousins. It is hard to enter or leave a city any other way than on a big road or some other crowded thoroughfare, and you will need to use extra caution in these moments.

We *always* wear **helmets**, even if we are just going around the block. We urge you to do so, too. You won't see a lot of helmets on cyclists in Italy—machismo is very much the order of the day—so it may take some extra effort on your part to put it on every day. For our part, we are happy to choose safety over machismo. We have seen too many injuries that could have easily been prevented by simply strapping on a helmet.

The same goes for *eye protection*. We always wear sunglasses, even on short rides. You never know when a stray bug is going to fly your way, so it pays to be prepared. Wraparound glasses or goggles are the best, because of the increased protection against wind and glare. Wind is hard on eyes, because evolution did not foresee that we would be rushing through space against the air for hours at a time. Glare is a major source of end-of-the-day headaches, so anything you can do to cut it down is to your advantage. Some of the new sunglass technology is absolutely incredible, much better than anything that was available just a few years ago. We recently upgraded our old goggles to the new wraparound Oakley's, and were amazed at the difference they made.

Mirrors have also come to be important to us. The great advantage of a rearview mirror is that you don't have to keep whipping your head around to see what's coming up behind you. This prevents stiff necks the next morning as well as simply being more efficient. A glance in the mirror takes much less time than craning the neck around, and you run less danger of missteering your bike while looking back. We personally think rearview mirrors are real lifesavers, so we urge you to try them out.

DAILY MAINTENANCE

We have found that if we will pay our bikes just a few minutes of attention each day, they will reward us with hours of service. Neglect those few minutes, however, and look out. Many of the safety problems people have on bike rides come from not noticing little things that need a tiny bit of adjusting. An improperly tightened quick release or a worn brake cable can make a very large difference in your well-being.

Before our first solo tour, we spent an evening at a bike shop learning the fundamentals of bike repair and adjustment. One evening was all that it took to learn enough basics to get by. We carry a couple of miniature repair books with us for minor adjustments (one of the best is Rob Van Der Plas's *Roadside Bicycle Repairs*, published by Kampman; $3.95). Anything more complicated goes to a bike shop. Before riding each day, we always make the following quick checks:

Quick releases: We make sure they are tightened down properly, having learned the hard way that bicycle gremlins can loosen these gadgets while you sleep.

Tire pressure: A squeeze will tell you whether you have the right amount of air in your tire. Keeping tires inflated to their right amount will prevent such common problems as pinched (snake-bit) tubes, as well as keeping you rolling down the road most efficiently.

Brakes: We take a look at the cable to make sure it's still in good shape, then squeeze the brakes a few times to be sure they are grabbing. When bikes come out of the hands of the airlines, the brakes always seem to need a little adjusting. During a tour, brakes seem to need attention every couple of days.

Chains: Keep 'em lubricated. A tube of Tri-Flow has accompanied us all over the world. There are probably other excellent products that do the same thing, but this is the one we always use. A drop on each chain link does it, and should be repeated every few days on a long tour. When your chain gets shiny, it's time for more. We change chains about once a year, more often if it has been a heavy travel year.

Handlebars: Give them a twist in all the relevant directions before you start each day. After having the unsettling but attention-focusing experience of having handlebars come off in our hands a couple of times, we now test them by giving them a heroic pull up, down, and sideways before riding off.

Derailleurs: We like to shift our gears up and down a few times in the first few minutes of a ride to be sure they are functioning smoothly. Adjustment of derailleurs is one of the facts of life in the saddle, so you might as well do it early in the day.

Seat height and angle: Once you get your seat at the right height and angle you probably will not have to bother with it again. It is worth checking it each day, however, because many sore knees, shoulders, and numb crotches are the result of improper seat adjustment. Get a good bike shop to show you just how to position your seat and its angle to give you the most efficient and comfortable stroke.

WARMING UP

We have found that our touring day goes much more smoothly if we take a few minutes to stretch before riding, and then take it easy the first mile or two. We have developed a simple routine which we will share with you.

Warming up is sometimes hard to remember because you will often be excited about getting off on the day's ride. It has been our experience that many of the common complaints, such as aching knees at the end of the day, are the result of starting off too quickly without a warm-up. The joints of the body contain material that is designed to cushion shock and friction, but to do so efficiently it must be warm. The reason is that the material expands when it is warm, and it is the expansion that gives it its cushioning power. Just as your pillow needs fluffing in the morning after being slept on overnight, your joints need some "fluffing" to get the night's flatness and stiffness out of them. The following stretches will warm your joints slowly and gently. Your first few minutes on the bike should also be slow and gentle. We make it a practice to spin around for five or ten minutes first if we have to tackle a big hill first thing in the morning. The older you are, the more important your warm-up is. Both of us are in our forties, but since learning to stretch and warm up properly, we have never missed a day's touring because of soreness or injury. Here are the four easy stretches that we have evolved over the years. We are by no means experts on stretching; these exercises have simply worked for us. If you would like a more formal series of bike stretches, read Bob Anderson's thorough book on the subject, *Stretching* (Shelter Publications; $9.95).

Stretch No. 1: Lie on your back on the floor. Bring your knees up and clasp your arms around them. Breathe deeply and slowly as you rock gently around, massaging your lower back. Keep your stomach muscles relaxed; induce the rocking motion with your hands. Continue for a minute or two, until the lower back and sacral area feels warmed up, then stretch out and relax for a little while.

Stretch No. 2: Sit on the floor with your legs stretched out in front of you. Place your hands on your thighs. As you breathe out slowly, lean forward and slide your hands down your legs as far as is comfortable for you. As you breathe in, slide your hands back up your legs. Repeat for a minute or two, in coordination with your breathing. Each time you slide down your legs with your hands, you may notice you go a little farther, although please avoid making a contest out of it.

Stretch No. 3: Lie on your stomach, propping yourself up on your elbows. Breathing slowly and deeply, raise each leg in turn 3 or 4 inches off the floor. Do these lifts slowly and gently, raising the legs just a few inches and then lowering them.

Stretch No. 4: Take your right hand and grip your left shoulder. Breathing slowly and deeply, turn your head gently from side to side. Turn first toward the side you are holding,

STRETCH NO. 1

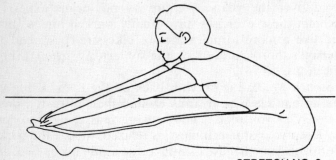

STRETCH NO. 2

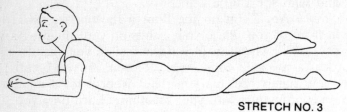

STRETCH NO. 3

STRETCH NO. 4

then 180 degrees the other direction (or as much as is comfortable). Repeat three times, then switch your grip to the opposite shoulder. After three repetitions, pause in the middle and slowly look up and down three times.

BREATHING FOR PEAK ENDURANCE

Efficient breathing is essential to feeling good at the end of the touring day. Nature has handed us an obstacle to overcome in this department. When people get upset or are under stress, they tend to breathe from the chest instead of from the abdomen. This fires off the adrenaline machinery, the three-million-year-old fight or flight response. Adrenaline is a powerful stimulant, but it is designed for short bursts only. It is important to stay relaxed and centered as you ride, so that your breathing can stay deep in your abdomen as well as your chest. When the breathing is only up in the chest, the heart has to work harder and the blood pressure goes up.

Most of the blood circulation in your lungs is in the lower third, between the bottom of your sternum and your navel. Over a quart of blood circulates down there every minute, as compared with less than a teacup up at the top of your lungs, just below your collarbone. Many of us keep our bellies tight, forcing the breath up into the chest. Our bodies will work much more efficiently if we can learn to relax our bellies. If there was only one piece of advice that we could give to make riding more fun, it would be to keep the belly relaxed so that you can breathe deeply down into your abdomen as well as up in your chest. That way, you will be using all the area that nature has provided. If you would like a tape that details efficient breathing activities, you can send for one that Gay has recorded (*The Art of Breathing and Centering*, available from your favorite bookstore or from Audio Renaissance, 5858 Wilshire Boulevard, Suite 205, Los Angeles, CA 90036; $9.95).

PART TWO

THE TOURS

Our Price Ranges

As in our tour books of France and the U.K., we have used a general guide to the prices of lodging and dining. For lodging, a Modest designation means two people can spend the night for less than $50; a Medium rating puts the hotel in the $50–100 category; a Top designation means that a double will cost in excess of $100. For dining, a Modest designation means that two people can have a meal and a glass of wine apiece for less than $25; a Medium designation goes to those restaurants where it will cost $25–50 for the equivalent meal; a Top designation means that the meal and wine will be in excess of $50. Naturally, heartier appetites and especially a fondness for *vino* by the bottle rather than the glass will escalate the prices sharply.

Note: Because all street signs in Italy use kilometers, we have given distances in kilometers in this book. For conversion purposes, 1 mile = 1.609 kilometers, 1 kilometer = .621 miles.

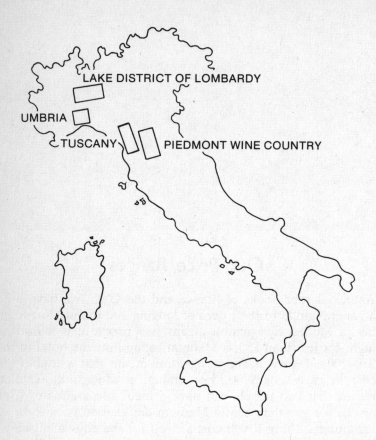

LAKE DISTRICT OF LOMBARDY

UMBRIA

TUSCANY

PIEDMONT WINE COUNTRY

THE LAKE DISTRICT OF LOMBARDY

WE HAVE CHOSEN THE LAKE DISTRICT FOR OUR FIRST TOUR for several reasons. First, it is easily accessible from Milan's Malpensa Airport, which is one of the two airports that the international visitor is likely to use to get into Italy. Actually, Malpensa is 30 miles outside of Milan in the direction of the Lake District; for that reason we are using it as the jumping-off place for the tour. Second, the Lake District is an ideal tour to use to get into shape if you are going to be taking the other tours in the book. The terrain, by and large, is flat, except for one day of hilly challenges. We have found that it takes about three days for us to get toughened up for touring, even if we think we are in shape. You will find that the early stages of the Lake District tour are forgiving. Third, the Lake District has some of the most splendid scenery of any place we have been in Europe. No wonder the area has drawn visitors for hundreds of years. Touring the Lake District has a special feel to it—you may think you are back in the nineteenth century. The same grand hotels that royalty stayed in a hundred years ago are still here and now, in a more egalitarian era, are open to all.

Here you will see people strolling along promenades at lakeside or heading off in packs to hike the nearby hills. Visitors spend hours at outdoor cafés, sipping cappuccino while listening to the slap of the gentle waves against the shore. We think the two best lakes for cycling are Como and Maggiore, so we do not route this tour over to Lake Garda. Should you wish to extend your tour of the Lake District you could easily get over to Garda in a day, though we have found that car traffic makes Garda a less appealing riding experience than the other two lakes.

Como and Maggiore: this is bicycle touring at its best. You will see why Stendhal said that Como possessed "everything noble, everything evoking love." It is a gorgeous, deep blue, this lake that another poet called the "looking glass of Venus." Known as Larius to the ancient Romans, Como later was discovered by the aristocracy. They built the gardens and villas that still surround the lake. The larger Lake Maggiore has shores in both Italy and Switzerland. Our tour winds in and out of both countries, finding a few back roads that will get you away from the crowds. The views around Maggiore are unparalleled. The towering mountains surround the lake, allowing the eye to wander back and forth between grandeur and stillness.

Although the climate in this region is generally mild, the weather is quite changeable. Last time we rode through the Lake District we had absolutely gorgeous weather for the first couple of days, then a spell of misty rain and cold. It was early June, though, still a bit early for this northern area. September and October are probably the ideal times to tour this region, both for the weather and because the hordes of tourists will have mostly gone home.

In the introductory sections of other tours we give a bit of information on the cuisine of the region. The Lake District does not have such a distinctive cuisine as Piedmont, Tuscany, or Umbria. Probably this is due to the centuries of catering to travelers, trying to please English, German, French, and of course, Italian visitors. You can get just about anything you want here, though, and the food is uniformly good. We cannot remember any meal in this region that was less than excellent. Some fondly remembered dining experiences include: *gnocchi* (potato dumplings) with a light Gorgonzola sauce up in the Swiss part of Lake Maggiore, some fine fresh trout prepared with a simple garlic butter sauce, and a *cannelloni* dish with a side of fried squash blossoms and truffles. If you like liver and onions—we do—this dish is easy to find in the Lake District. Also, there are countless outdoor lakeside cafés serving exotic ice cream creations along with coffee and alcoholic drinks.

Ready? Let's go.

DAY ONE: MALPENSA TO STRESA

(50 kilometers for the day; easy)
The Lake District of Italy has much in common with the Lake District in England. For generations their shores have harbored poets and artists who come to seek the sweep of light and the change in the face of the lakes with time and season. Both have developed rich traditions of tourism, with villas and luxury hotels alongside private homes and campgrounds. And both offer magnificent vistas wherever you venture. We found the Italian Lake District to have a more Alpine feeling, although we're sure you'll notice the tremendous variety of scenery. The friendly people, ease of the roads, and unlimited visual pleasures make this a cyclist's dream, and a great introduction to Italy.

Note: Today's journey is part functional—to get you to the Lake District—and part scenic (once you get there). The first half of the trip is a little less than scenic, but the lakes make up for it. You'll move first through the most heavily industrialized area in Italy on the most efficient route we found, then be rewarded with the endless beauty of the lakes for the remainder of the tour.

We start with an easy day, mostly flat and a relatively short distance. If you are anything like us, you'll like to follow a long transoceanic flight with an easy day. If you can start this tour on a day other than Sunday you'll probably be happier, as this road is busy with recreational excursions on the weekend.

This tour takes a short hop into Switzerland for the second night. It will give you an interesting opportunity to contrast the folkways and attitudes of these vastly different countries that converge at Lake Maggiore.

Communication is easy throughout the Lake District. We stopped to pick up a map and found that all the clerks spoke at least four languages. Except for certain drivers and most motorcyclists, people in the Lake District tend to be helpful and polite. This is especially true if you do your cycle touring in May or June. In July or August tourist services are stretched to the limit; by September, though the crowds have departed, many service personnel have lost their taste for the general public.

As you exit Malpensa Airport, you will see a sign directing you to Somma. Like many Italian roads, it is not marked with a number. Although it is fairly busy with car traffic, there is a bike lane down the right side of the road. There is a sign about ¼ mile on saying SS336. In less than a mile you will come to a fork.

Take the right toward Somma and Lake Maggiore. Here you will get your first taste of the wooded scenery that abounds in the Lake District. You will also experience your first windy bypassing of the famous Italian car speedsters. The road is level and fairly smooth. Don't be surprised to see Italians out on bikes in large groups. After 3½ kilometers, there is a moderate uphill climb into the town of **Somma**.

Proceed through Somma on the main thoroughfare. As you leave Somma there is a long downhill run, with a high stone wall on the right, then a flat stretch.

Follow the sign straight ahead toward Sesto Calende. This short section is semi-industrial, but wide enough for both bikes and cars. Continue following the signs to Sesto Calende.

At the Y fork, go left toward Sesto Calende.

Through the next intersection, keep following the directions toward Sesto. You'll begin to see red tile roofs and more open fields along this level road. Sesto Calende has a reputable museum with an extensive collection of artifacts from the Golasecca culture from the excavation of important nearby Iron Age tombs. A tenth-century church just north of town houses well-preserved frescoes and a big crypt.

On the far side of Sesto Calende, which is 15 kilometers from Malpensa, go straight toward Sempione and Arona at the fork. You'll cross a bridge over the river and come to a stoplight.

Go right toward Arona. (Sign: 9 k to Arona)
The road continues to be primarily level and wooded, with businesses along the roadside.

Continue toward Stresa. Shortly after this right fork, you'll get a fleeting glimpse of one of Europe's treasured spots, Lake Maggiore. This is the preferred road for tourists, and the number of signs and shops confirms it. (roughly 21 kilometers from airport to Dormelletto).

As you enter **Arona**, after 9 kilometers from the stoplight turn, you'll ride under a long line of trees and by pastel houses. When we passed through here there was a street fair and the roads were teeming with pedestrians, as well as cars.

On a typical day, Arona is a great place to sit and view this gorgeous lake, especially from the long park adjacent to lakeside. You have an excellent view from here of the Rocca de Angera. Arona was a refuge for escapees from the destruction of Milan in the twelfth century and the pawn of the dukes of Lombardy for centuries. As a result, its well-preserved old city has several sights you may want to sample before continuing up the lake. The gothic portico to the fifteenth-century governor's mansion is especially striking, and there are also two fine churches with historical paintings and an enormous statue here.

As you exit Arona, you'll have a sharp uphill climb onto

the main road to Stresa. Even on a Sunday, official Italian touring day, the road is relatively uncrowded and wide enough for you and the Italians. Many lovely villas and lakeside resorts line the lake, and the occasional beach welcomes you.

You have the option here to take a challenging climb up into Ghevio, where the ruins of a thirteenth-century castle huddle on Massino Visconti; you rejoin the main road at Lesa. Our route will follow the unparalleled beauty of the lakeside avenue.

On your way to Stresa, you'll pass through **Meina**, a lakeside resort with fine old homes and estates. The road is mainly flat and smooth as you enter **Lesa**, where the density of foliage increases and the road winds right next to the lake. There are stately homes on the hill, an opportunity for swimming, and a picturesque harbor on the right, then the road turns into a slight upgrade for about ½ mile as you leave Lesa. Hotels and restaurants abound in this popular area, framed by centuries-old pines, poplars, and other trees. The area is impeccably clean and extremely pleasant. In the health resort of **Bilgirate** another harbor hugs the lakeside. There are many spots where you'll be tempted to stop and fill your eyes with the splendor of the lake. The next stretch of road is less built up and gives you a panoramic view of the length of Lago Maggiore. Terraced gardens front the old homes to the left, and trees grow right down to the lake's shores. An ancient stone wall appears on the left, and several ferries loaded with tourists cruise along near the shore. A large parking area signals your entrance into **Stresa**.

WHERE TO STAY AND DINE IN STRESA

Our recommendation in Stresa is the Hotel Milan e Speranza au Lac (piazza Imbarcadero 28049 Stresa-Italia; tel. [0323]31178 or 31190). This hotel overlooks the main promenade and is located directly on the lake shore. The Milan au Lac is gracious and well-appointed, and its employees definitely of the old school. (Top)

If you want something less fancy but still very comfortable, we can recommend the Hotel Sempione (or Simplon), which is also on the main lakeside promenade (lungolago 28049 Stresa; tel. [0323]30463). The rooms come with bath and breakfast. (Medium)

There are several luxury hotels past the main promenade of town. If your taste and pocketbook run toward a more spacious and ornate setting for the evening, you may want to try the Regina Palace, where many celebrities have rested over the years (lungolago Umberto I no. 27, 28049 Stresa; tel. [0323]30171). The Regina boasts a striking architectural design, elaborate columns, marble staircase, and swimming pool. Many rooms, all of which are fully appointed, have excellent views of the lake and Borromean Islands.

A favorite with the locals is the Albergo Ristorante "Luina." It's been here for years, it's always packed, and its excellent local reputation is well deserved (tel. 30285). The Luina features a range of pasta and regional specialities, including herbed sole and handmade ravioli. (Modest–Medium)

There are many other restaurants in Stresa, located both along the promenade and in the central square, a couple of blocks along the bricked lanes away from the lakeside. In the central square area, we liked the Ristorante Piemontese, which has a menu in four languages. They had two of our favorites on the menu: *gnocchi* with a cheese sauce and *tagliatelle* with the wondrous local mushroom, known here as *porcini* (in France called *cepes*). (Medium)

WHAT TO SEE AND DO IN STRESA

The main amusement in Stresa, practiced by both locals and visitors alike, is strolling. The lakeside will be thronged morning and evening with happy promenaders, pausing occasionally to lick an ice cream (*gelato*) or sip a cappuccino. Swimming is an option along here, and if you wish to speed across the waters, you can take one of the many boat tours that leave from the center of town. The Isola Bella (beautiful island) is visible from Stresa, and its castle and elaborate terraced gardens can be visited by boat.

Stresa is home to a famous international music festival each August, and has tennis, horseback riding, yachting, and swimming readily available. It also houses a lovely botanical garden and small zoo including pheasants, kangaroos, and ostriches as residents. Stresa reached the height of its development as a resort in the nineteenth century, and you'll notice the influence of that era in the architecture and tone of the town.

DAILY SUMMARY

LAKE DISTRICT TOUR: DAY ONE

Malpensa to Stresa

(50 kilometers; easy)

As you exit Malpensa Airport, you will see a sign directing you to Somma. Like many Italian roads, it is not marked with a number. Although it is fairly busy with car traffic, there is a bike lane down the right side of the road. There is a sign about ¼ mile along saying SS336. In less than a mile you will come to a fork.

- Take the right toward Somma and Lake Maggiore. After 3½ kilometers, there is a moderate uphill climb into the town of Somma.
- Proceed through Somma on the main thoroughfare.
- Follow the sign straight ahead toward Sesto Calende.
- At the Y fork, go left toward Sesto Calende.
- Through the next intersection, keep following the directions toward Sesto.
- On the far side of Sesto Calende, which is 15 kilometers from Malpensa, go straight toward Sempione and Arona at the fork.
- Go right toward Arona (Sign: 9 k. to Arona).
- Continue toward Stresa. (Roughly 21 kilometers from airport to Dormelletto.)

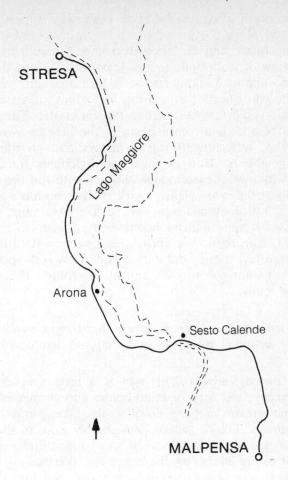

DAY TWO: STRESA TO LOCARNO

(55 kilometers for the day; easy)
Regarding lunch: there are an endless number of cafés and
restaurants along the route. We are not recommending a
lunch stop as you will undoubtedly find your own special place
as you ride.

Exit Stresa north along the lakeside road. The supersplurge hotels spread along the lake from town center, and include the Regina Palace and Des Iles Borromées. You'll have an excellent view of Isola Bella as you leave Stresa. You'll come into **Baveno** almost 3 kilometers after Stresa, where we were happy to be going north through this important tourist center. On a bicycle you'll fare better than the car traffic. The architecture of the area is a combination of the best of Swiss and French styles, reflecting its mixed history and proximity to northern neighbors. Iron railings and balconies frame the shuttered windows of pastel stucco houses with red tile roofs. Signs for local shops are clearly marked. Baveno has a tourist information office at lakeside. There are swimming pools, campsites, and many natural nooks and crannies to explore just off the main road. We chose this direction for the tour because it has less traffic, and the lakeside view is so spectacular we didn't want you to miss any of the route's charms by taking side roads.

Six and a half kilometers from Stresa, head right toward Locarno. This section of road is more functional than decorative.

Go right toward Verbania. The way is a little rougher here through a more rustic area of small homes and businesses, with marshes and streams ambling down to the lake. Many homes are built into the hillside, which rises sharply close to the lake in places. You'll see back across the lake toward Stresa as you wind closer to the lake's edge here and into **Verbania**.

Verbania is actually a composite town. Neighbors Intra and Pallanza joined forces in 1939 to create Verbania. For that reason, the town retains a pleasing split personality. Pallanza, which faces the sea, carries the aristocratic resort face for the city, while Intra has developed more industry in addition to its tourist zone.

At the light here, go right toward Suna and Pallanza. (sign: Zona Turista) Well-cared-for homes and trees frame the street, while parks and cafés cluster lakeside. Two museums and two churches, one Renaissance and one romanesque, can be visited in this area.

Follow Zona Turista signs to stay along the lake. If you packed your racket, there are some beautifully maintained tennis courts along here, as well as piers from which to fish and cafés to enjoy another morning espresso. Tiny harbors sit next to beautifully maintained parks.

Go right toward Intra at this fork. Ivy-covered walls lead you into a gentle uphill, our first today, for a short grade which quickly becomes level again. You can stop and tour the harmoniously laid-out gardens and fountains of the Villa Taranto here before rejoining 34 to your right.

Take the signs toward Locarno in busy Intra. The buildings here, made of light pastel stone, have a quaint Italian flavor, with a more rustic feeling. You'll glide into a particularly beautiful stretch of the road where the passage is sometimes narrow. We noticed throughout this tour that the locals are very respectful of bicyclists.

(*Note to those looking for a challenge:* At intervals along this section, you can take steeper roads to the small villages higher in the hills, then wind back down to the lake. Otherwise, follow the signs to Locarno.)

The road remains level and fairly smooth. The upper part of the lake opens to view now as the scenery becomes less populated for a stretch of several miles. A rare swimming area appears just before **Oggebbio** and a particularly lush foliage-covered stretch of rock. A section of rough road passes some lakeside tennis courts. The cycling is very easy except for the problem of keeping your eyes on the road. Frequent stops should solve that problem. You'll pass **Cannero Riviera** through more deeply wooded and wonderfully scented arches of chestnut and beech trees and flowering bushes on a slight upgrade.

Continue toward Locarno through this beautiful array of red tile roofs and flowering bushes on the hill and shore. The road

narrows here and presents a viewing stop where we passed a
resting cyclist. He was studying the Castelli di Cannero just
off the shore, a stone ruin of two medieval castles with waves
lapping its rounded rock. When we were there last, the road
had just been repaved and we glided along the more winding
road passing many recreational cyclists enjoying the perfect
weather.

There are several places to stop and drink in the view of
mountains and boats. People have obviously treasured this
area for centuries, and the terraced homes reflect their pride.
The landscape turns more rugged here, although your course
remains smooth and basically level. The first view of **Cannobio**, especially late in the afternoon, is a palette of pastels
and tiers of houses, accompanied by church bells and singing
birds. Prepare yourself for a rattling 2-block cobblestone ride
through this well-developed tourist center, which sponsors an
annual fish festival in July. Next you'll ease into a tree-lined
stretch as the mountains open in a pass through the steeply
rugged Cannobina Valley to your left. The road grade veers
slightly upward and the terrain becomes more mountainous.
Rocks have been used to form walls high up the hill in places.

You'll need your passports to cross into Switzerland,
where the guards are friendly and casual. A sidewalk appears
along with the more austere facades of buildings. In **Brissago**,
the promenade of hotels begins again, with a distinctly Swiss
air. The snow-covered mountains are visible in the distant
north. The combination of thick trees, pink houses dotting
the hillside and the gentle rhythms of the lake are soothing
and stimulating at the same time. We stopped on the spot to
vote this our favorite place in Europe. You'll pass through
Porto Ronco, another pleasant village built up the side of the
mountain. Ascona can be seen as you bend around the well-
manicured road, still complete with sidewalk. Rock outcroppings overhang the road, and some enviable homes nestle
under the cliffs at water's edge.

The highway narrows along the stone cliffs as you approach Ascona, and signs warn of falling rocks. Greenery appears on every possible surface, and the cool mountain

breezes refresh you as you pedal. A mile-long tunnel with sidewalk leads under the mountain and to a junction.

Follow the sign at the fork toward Locarno.

After approximately ½ mile, follow the Centro sign. The signs here are also painted on the street and hard to miss.

Turn left at the next stoplight.

WHERE TO STAY AND DINE IN LOCARNO

Our best recommendation is to stay in a lovely hotel just this side of Locarno, called the Hotel Arancio. It's in the town of Ascona (CH-6612 Ascona TI; tel. [093]352333). You'll see the sign for it on the left as you enter the outskirts of Locarno. There is a steep little climb of a block to get to the hotel, but once you arrive, you'll be greeted by easygoing staff members, large rooms with commanding balcony views of the lake, and reasonable prices. You can arrange to eat all meals here or just breakfast, which is a buffet of sensational chewy bread, cheeses, and yogurt. (Medium)

If you want to stay in the heart of Locarno, follow the signs that say Centro as you enter Locarno. The Hotel Dell'Angelo is located at one end of the central square (piazza Grande, CH-6601 Locarno; tel. [093]318175). You can sit on the rooftop terrace and enjoy a good view of the old city and the cobblestone plaza below. The restaurant on the ground floor serves a fine pizza, as well as other regional specialities. When we were last there, they had just renovated the rooms, elevating the prices. (Medium)

There are also many lakeside hotels in Muralto, the signs for which are near the downtown area.

This city, like most around Lake Maggiore, abounds with good food in all price ranges. According to your mood, you can snack or feast in a wide range of styles and moods. If you want to see how the other half lives, have dinner up the hill at the Grand Hotel Locarno. (Top)

WHAT TO SEE AND DO IN LOCARNO

The tourist information office here is on via F. Balli 2 (tel. 318633), which will provide you with a wide range of recreational and sightseeing opportunities. From the main square to the public gardens and old town, Locarno has many pleasures to offer the visitor.

DAILY SUMMARY

LAKE DISTRICT TOUR: DAY TWO

Stresa to Locarno

(55 kilometers; easy)

- Exit Stresa north along the lakeside road.
- Three kilometers from Stresa, head right toward Locarno.
- Go right toward Verbania.
- At the light here in Verbania, go right toward Suna and Pallanza (sign: Zona Turista).
- Follow Zona Turista signs to stay along the lake.
- Go right toward Intra at this fork.
- Take the signs toward Locarno in busy Intra.
- Continue toward Locarno through this beautiful array of red tile roofs and flowering bushes on the hill and shore.
- Follow the sign at the fork toward Locarno.
- After approximately ½ mile, follow the Centro sign.
- Turn left at the next stoplight.

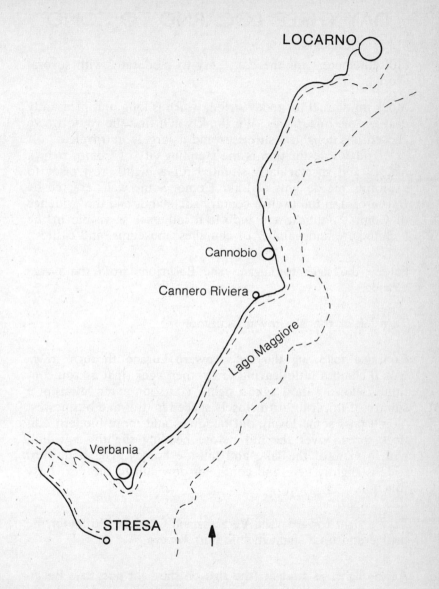

LOCARNO

Cannobio

Cannero Riviera

Lago Maggiore

Verbania

STRESA

DAY THREE: LOCARNO TO COMO

(100 kilometers for the day; easy to moderate, with several short hills)

Stock up on fuel for today's ride, which is long, but pleasantly easy on the quadriceps. We think you'll find the route we've chosen has delightful surprises and is largely untraveled.

Today's destination is the stunning city of Como, rich in history and spectacularly situated for a night's rest prior to exploring the delights of Lake Como. Some walls erected by Barbarossa in the twelfth century still stand, and the evidence of Como's political and industrial influence is visible in the architecture and number of churches, museums, and castles.

Follow the signs to Lugano and Bellinzona from the piazza Grande.

Turn left at the lake toward Lugano.

Continue following the signs toward Lugano through town. You'll climb a little leaving town, then veer right as you continue following the Lugano signs. You soon enter **Minusio**, a suburb of Locarno, with closely spaced houses and businesses. You'll pass some lovely old buildings and more modern edifices spread over the hill before heading slightly downhill, with a view of the lake and hillside homes. The boulevard widens slightly here and continues downhill to the next busy junction.

Take a right toward Valle Verzacsa and Gordola. Go under the bridge and up a slight incline into **Tenero**.

At the light, go straight (the sign on the light post says Bellinzona). This less trafficked road takes you through the old city. Keep following the signs toward Bellinzona through the town. Many of the buildings are vine-covered or flower-bedecked,

although much of the route here is industrial. We have tried
to keep you off the main car route.

In **Riazzino**, about 10 kilometers outside Locarno, go right toward Lugano (and several other towns). Our morning's plan is
to cut across the top of the lake and head back toward Luino.

After about 2 kilometers, turn left toward Luino. This fertile
agricultural land is very flat and dotted with trees.

Over the bridge head right toward Luino. You ride along the
foot of the hills here, passing through **Maggadino**, a small
village of rustic houses. The roadway on this side of the lake
has a rougher surface, but far less traffic than the more developed resorts across the water. Grapes and vegetables terrace
the hills, and the architecture may remind you of Alsace, with
the flowers in window boxes and old stone facades. Stay on the
main road, which is rather bumpy but basically level. You'll
continue to pass through small villages, some of which are not
marked. Boats bob anchored close to shore and trees overhang the road.

Continue following the signs toward Luino, which takes you
directly along the shore. Although basically level, the highway
has a few slight rises. You may see the train speeding along
above you on the hill. Vines and flowers flow down the stone
walls.

About 25 kilometers or so from Locarno, you'll cross the border again into Italy. Interestingly, immediately over the border
the houses are more colorful. Pastels reappear, and the course
gets smoother and widens. The scenery here is lush and thick,
with no buildings for several miles, then the occasional house.
You have a continual view across the lake, depending on the
weather. This is good riding territory, peaceful and uncrowded. You'll pass a swimming area on the beach about 8
kilometers from the border crossing, but otherwise this stretch
is a nature lover's paradise. You'll pass under three tunnels
into **Maccagno**, a small village with narrow lanes.

Go right toward Luino at the fork. You'll pass through a series of tunnels, with the elevated train rail to your left, and then through the small and charming town of **Colmegna**, where you may want to pause and admire an ideal rural Italian town. Civilization reappears in the larger town of **Luino**, where there are several outdoor cafés along the lake. Also, the promenade is shaded with large trees that make an ideal setting for a picnic lunch.

If you want a more sumptuous repast on this longer day, we can recommend the restaurant Due Scale, which is on the piazza della Libertà 30 (tel. 530396). If you come through any day but Friday, you can enjoy unusual cuisine, such as risotto with frog, or a large variety of regional specialities and fresh fish in this restored eighteenth-century building.

At the far end of town, turn left at the sign to Ponte Tresa (and Lugano).

After a block, go left over the cobblestones toward Lugano. The ride passes through the town's interesting section of shops.

Head right at the roundabout toward Lugano. You twine along a slight uphill through town, the first real hill of the day.

Continue toward Lugano after several blocks of residential area. A dam on your right blocks the placid river, where rounded trees create an impressionistic painting in the water's reflection. The grade is slightly uphill after about 6 kilometers, and stoplights direct you through the tunnel under the hill. This section of the ride is wooded and rural as you come into **Cremenaga**.

Go straight toward Ponte Tresa at this junction. The route leans uphill in this virtually deserted area, with little villages off each side and glorious green all around. You're on a back lane here with a bubbling brook on your left and ferns crowding the road to your right. After about 10 kilometers the woodland opens into the fairly large town of **Ponte Tresa**.

Follow the signs to Porto Ceresio. The south end of Lake Lugano appears to your left, a very tidy and elegant landscape. The road is essentially flat and hugs the lake all the way to Porto Ceresio. A low stone wall separates you from the lake, and the narrow road is bordered by stone cliffs on the right. Birdsong accompanies your ride all day, not masked by heavy traffic.

In Brusimpiano, go straight, following the signs to Porto Ceresio (on the left hand side of the road). You won't encounter much here except beautiful scenery in all directions. Houses dot the hillside across the lake. About 10 kilometers from Ponte Tresa you come into **Porto Ceresio**, an important holiday resort and busy entrance to Switzerland.

Go left toward Varese at the fork.

Follow the narrow lanes left into the *centro*. This beautiful little town has a couple of outdoor cafés and nestles like a little jewel on the lake's edge. You'll continue on around the lake and into Switzerland again, where you'll be greeted for some reason by an unusual number of gas stations. The stone walls are darker here, and the homeowners cultivate vibrantly colored flowers. The way remains basically level, with an uphill just after the border crossing. The view across the lake is breathtaking. Swans cruise by the shore, and some homes are built on piers directly over the water. We passed fishermen leisurely enjoying the afternoon and several lakeside cafés. Another small rise brings you into **Riva San Vitale**, 35 kilometers from Luino.

At the fork, go right toward Rancate. The street through this small town opens into residential areas and terraced hillsides. As you leave town there is a small upward incline.

At the hill's top go right toward Rancate. This section of greenhouses and businesses is intended to avoid the main roads. A moderate climb brings you into woodlands and a view across the valley. About 3½ kilometers brings you into **Rancate**, a small town with narrow lanes.

At the junction, go straight across toward Mendrisio.

Turn left after a block toward Mendrisio.

Follow the signs across the *autostrada*.

In Mendrisio, follow the signs toward Chiasso. You are on the outskirts of a big city here, taking the back roads in. Continue following the signs toward Chiasso. New buildings are side by side with the old city. The hills reappear to your right as you begin heading downhill. After about 3½ kilometers, you'll pass through **Balerna**.

Follow the sign winding right toward Chiasso. As you continue downhill, the valley and busier roads are visible on your right.

At the light, go toward Chiasso. Stay on the road marked in blue to avoid the *autostrada*.

At the roundabout, go more or less straight across toward Como and Chiasso.

At the next intersection, go right toward Como Centro.

Follow the signs through the next intersection toward Como. You'll come into Italy again through a border crossing, with a sign Como hanging overhead.

Follow the signs toward Centro. Your last moderate but rather long climb takes you into **Como** proper. This is a large city, and you may need patience coming into such a busy place after your quiet day.

Follow the road straight toward Bergamo, where the road turns and heads downhill. A sign to your left coming through the intersection says Centro. This is quite an exhilarating downhill past more cultivated yards, huge old trees, and finally cobble-stone and shops. You'll see a fleeting glimpse of Lake Como to your left between the closely spaced buildings.

Keep following the signs toward Centro.

At the light, go left toward Centro Città. Wind your way through the one-way streets of the city of Como, where you'll stop for the night. The moment you get to Como you'll be glad you arrived on a bicycle. This beautiful city has a parking problem to rival that of Boston or San Francisco. Many peo-ple use Como as the jumping-off place for their explorations of the Lake District, so throughout the high season tourist services are stretched to the maximum. The location, nestled among the surrounding hills, will make you understand why it was the site of ancient revels. Como has been a prosperous city since Roman times, and shows no sign of letting up. Fa-mous as the silk capital of the world for centuries, Como also nestles in a particularly sensuous location at the southwest end of Lake Como, hailed since ancient times as the most beautiful in the world. Over the next two days you can make your own evaluation of what has been called a perfectly bal-anced jewel of lakes.

The cathedral here is worth exploring, being built com-pletely of marble. Check out the amazing facade. Both Pliny the Elder and Pliny the Younger came from Como; statues of both can be found in niches of the facade.

WHERE TO STAY AND DINE IN COMO

Just before heading uphill toward Bellagio, if you turn left along the lakefront, you'll find the hotel we enjoyed on our most recent visit. The Hotel Marco's (via Lungo Lario Trieste 62, 22100 Como; tel. [031]303470 or 303628) has immaculate rooms run by a very cordial staff. The beds were firm and to our liking and the bathroom large and well equipped. The hotel is behind their excellent restaurant, which serves a wide selection of fresh fish, as well as excellent pasta and local specialities. Nearby is the funicular station Como–Brunate, and the lakeside sidewalk offers romantic nighttime strolling with the twinkling lights of Como; all around. (Medium)

Another lakeside hotel is the Metropole Suisse Au Lac. (piazza Cavour 19, 22100 Como tel. [031]269444 or 266351). Rooms here are furnished with "period furniture" and have excellent views of the lake and the amenities of a four-star hotel. The great shopping area of Como and the cathedral are close by, as well as boat rides on Lake Como. (Top)

There are an unusually large number of cafés, trattorias, and full restaurants here, even by Italy's generous standards. If a lake view is preferred, try Da Pizzi, viale Geno 12 (tel. 266100; closed Thursdays). The Pizzi uses fresh regional produce and herbs in its innovative cuisine. (Medium–Top)

For the ambiance provided by an old inn, we recommend the Trattoria del Gesumin, via V. Giornate 44 (tel. 266030; closed Sundays). Here you can sample a mushroom omelet and fowl with herbs. (Top)

DAILY SUMMARY

LAKE DISTRICT TOUR: DAY THREE

Locarno to Como

(100 kilometers; easy to moderate, with several short hills)

- Follow the signs to Lugano and Bellinzona from the piazza Grande.
- Turn left at the lake toward Lugano.
- Continue following the signs toward Lugano through town.
- Take a right toward Valle Verzacsa and Gordola.
- Go under the bridge and up a slight incline into Tenero.
- At the light, go straight (the sign on the light post says Bellinzona.)
- In Riazzino, go right toward Lugano (and several other towns), about 10 kilometers outside Locarno.
- After about 2 kilometers, turn left toward Luino.
- Over the bridge head right toward Luino.

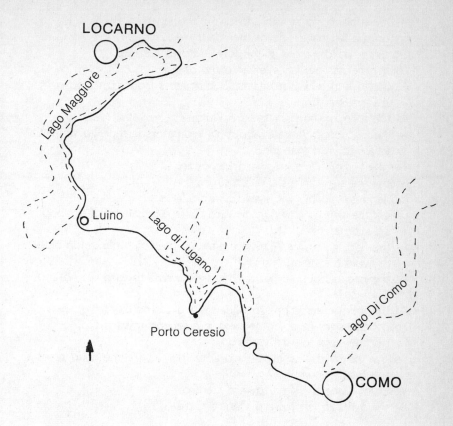

- Continue following the signs toward Luino, which takes you directly along the shore.
- About 25 kilometers or so from Locarno, you'll cross the border again into Italy.
- Go right toward Luino at the fork.
- At the far end of Luino, turn left at the sign to Ponte Tresa (and Lugano).
- After a block, go left over the cobblestones toward Lugano.
- Head right at the roundabout toward Lugano.
- Continue toward Lugano after several blocks of residential area.
- Go straight toward Ponte Tresa at this junction.
- Follow the signs to Porto Ceresio.

- In Brusimpiano go straight, following the signs to Porto Ceresio (on the left-hand side of the road).
- Go left toward Varese at the fork in Porto Ceresio.
- Follow the narrow lanes left into the *centro*.
- At the fork in Riva San Vitale, 35 kilometers from Luino, go right toward Rancate.
- At the hill's top go right toward Rancate.
- At the junction in Rancate, about 3½ kilometers farther, go straight across toward Mendrisio.
- Turn left after a block toward Mendrisio.
- Follow the signs across the *autostrada*.
- In Mendrisio, follow the signs toward Chiasso.
- Follow the sign winding right toward Chiasso in Balerna after about 3½ kilometers.
- At the light, go toward Chiasso. (Stay on the road marked in blue to avoid the *autostrada*.)
- At the roundabout, go basically straight across toward Como and Chiasso.
- At the next intersection, go right toward Como Centro.
- Follow the signs through the next intersection toward Como.
- Follow the signs toward Centro.
- Follow the road straight toward Bergamo, where the road turns and heads downhill.
- Keep following the signs toward Centro.
- At the light, go left toward Centro Città.

DAY FOUR: COMO TO BELLAGIO

(30 kilometers for the day; moderate hills)

Note: **Dress for visibility.** Today's itinerary takes you up the wilder and less traveled side of Lake Como to the world-famous resort of Bellagio. Blessed with one of the most awesome vantage points on the lake, Bellagio was built for the pleasure and convenience of visitors, and is both elegant and accessible. The route to day's end curves along the always magnificent coastline through a wide variety of landscape.

Start the day's ride with a climb out of Como on 1 toward Bellagio. After about 1 kilometer the road flattens out and views open along the lake. The homes along this part of the shore are very stately. You'll pass through a series of tunnels then wind down into the narrow lanes of the village of **Blevio**.

You turn slightly downhill here and pass by homes that have clearly been around for centuries. The stone walls, high on the right, low and sloping on the left, are well maintained, and vines cascade toward the street in many places. The scenery changes quickly from cultivated to wild, then back again. Just out of town you'll have a moderate climb of a little more than a mile. The road is very sinuous as the climb continues a little less steeply for approximately 3 kilometers total.

At the junction, follow the left fork downhill toward Bellagio. You have another short climb along snaking mountain roads where every bit of usable terrain is either inhabited or cultivated. You have a bird's-eye view across the lake to the homes on a lower elevation. Gray stone and pink stucco intermingle, and vegetation hovers over everything. Photo opportunities seem to be around every bend. Another climb, again moderate, takes you a further 1 kilometer or so and into more rugged countryside. In **Careno** the view is especially great. The passage continues to slope upward, then levels out. It is narrow, sometimes extremely, throughout.

Continue following the signs toward Bellagio. About 14 kilometers from Como, in **Nesso**, is a restaurant called the Three Roses, where you can get a good lunch to fuel you for the remaining ride. After lunch the terrain is wooded and studded with cliffs, and the road is relatively even for a while. You pass **Lezzeno** (a don't blink village) and roll into country again. In **Crotto**, you'll notice that every inch is tended and used. The countryside looks a little more rustic here, and many of the houses are constructed from old stone. Gardens flourish in the small spaces behind homes on the hill. A cemetery nestles beneath the road just before you come into **Rozzo**.

You'll climb a moderate hill through a heavily populated

area, then level out into a semirural area again. The grade is still up, but less steep. Deep glades and ferns protrude from the rock face, and many shades of green vie for attention. As you turn a corner you get a look at the primal cliff face off to the end of the point. The road widens slightly and feels more open. Your view across the lake is largely unobstructed throughout this part of the ride. A last short climb brings you into **Bellagio**.

Wind on the downhill run into the center of town. You have a wide choice of hotels for the night. To get to the best hotels, you'll have one last steep set of switchbacks, or else just follow the shorefront promenade.

Bellagio, known as "the pearl of the lake," deserves its reputation. It sits on a magnificent spot with Lake Lecco on one side and Lake Como on the other of its jutting promontory. There is a fine park here, the Villa Serbelloni, which is worth going through just to see the gardens. The information center above the central square is helpful if you want to take a deeper look at Bellagio and its environs. They have an up-to-date listing of all the hotels and restaurants, of which there are many in this much-visited town.

WHERE TO STAY AND DINE IN BELLAGIO

Bellagio has a large variety of rooms in all price ranges. The heart of the downtown area is dominated by the Hotel Excelsior Splendido (lungolago Manzoni 22021 Bellagio; tel. [031]950225). It's an old-fashioned hotel, but it has all the modern conveniences, including swimming pool and a pleasant dining room. Rooms for two, with bath, are in our Medium range. The hotel faces directly on the lake, where you can view cars and people coming off the boat ferry. (Medium)

There is a five-star hotel in town called the Grand Hotel Villa Serbelloni (via Roma 1, Bellagio CO; tel. [031]950216. It has its own private park and garden and has been taking good care of guests since 1872. It was in a look-but-don't touch category since we did not want to put quite that much of a dent in our credit cards, but if you have several hundred dollars a night to spend, this is definitely the best place in town. (Top)

Beautifully situated is the Albergo Ristorante "Il Perlo Panorama" (via Valassina 180; tel. [031]950229). It's a small hotel and a little off the beaten track, perfect for people whose priorities are quiet and a panoramic view. (Medium)

On one of the cobblestone streets in the center of town, look for the Ristorante Barchetta (salita Mella 13; tel. 951389). In addition to the usual range of pasta dishes, this restaurant specializes in locally caught fish. (Medium)

The Hotel Florence has a highly regarded dining room (tel. 950342). You might enjoy their smoked trout and their tricolor pasta in a creamy sauce made with local wild mushrooms. (Top)

For those interested in light food and café society, the entire lakeside promenade resembles one long open-air restaurant, dotted with unique gift shops and pastry tearooms.

DAILY SUMMARY

LAKE DISTRICT TOUR: DAY FOUR

Como to Bellagio

(30 kilometers; moderate hills)

Note: **Dress for visibility.**

- Start the day's ride with a climb out of Como on 1 toward Bellagio.
- At the junction after about 3 kilometers follow the left fork toward Bellagio and downhill.
- Continue following the signs toward Bellagio.

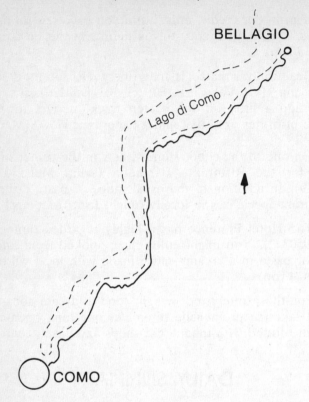

DAY FIVE: BELLAGIO TO COMO

(50 kilometers; easy to moderate)

Note: Today's ride contains an unlighted tunnel. You should have reflective patches on you and your bike. Also, bring a light.

    Today's return to Como samples the less frequented side of this promontory and Lake Lecco. We've done our best to avoid the heavily industrialized area around Lecco and to take you by back roads through the valley to Como.

Follow the road left toward Lecco. Just out of town the hill climbs sharply for about ½ kilometer, then forks.

Turn left toward Lecco. Head uphill again for a short way, then traverse the functional 2 blocks of town.

Turn right at the T fork toward Lecco. Up again, this time in steeper switchbacks for ½ kilometer.

Turn left toward Lecco and continue climbing, being sure to look back for the glorious view before cresting the hill. You roll downhill with Lago di Lecco visible between hedges to your left. After a downhill run of a couple of kilometers, the road twists up again slightly through a wooded glen with magnificent evergreens and wildflowers. Stay on the road toward Lecco. There are several great old buildings to match the majestic trees, and the view across the lake can be distracting. On some days the mist hangs like curling ribbons through the mountain passes. After 7 kilometers you will pass a small waterfall to your right, and the foliage crowds the road. You're riding fairly level now with an occasional downgrade. The high stone cliffs along this narrow passage are stunning, a mixture of rugged and delicate. The small village of **Vassena**, with its manicured gardens and well-tended homes, is followed by deeper woodlands and the closer sound of the lake's ripples. You are much nearer to the water's edge today than yesterday, although the pale stone cliffs jutting to your right are just as formidable. You enter **Oliveto** 11 kilometers from Bellagio.

Follow the road left toward Lecco. An enclosed harbor hugs the shore, while more unscalable cliffs rise behind. You'll cross narrow stone bridges and continue to have a view of the towns that grasp the shore of the lake. When we were there, a lone fisherman sat on a rock off the shore waiting for the fish. The road is overhung with trees at several points along this next wild section, as you look across at the busy metropolis of Mandello. Almost 16 kilometers from Bellagio, note that you'll encounter a serious tunnel. It has no lights and is quite dark and long. Bring a light to protect yourself. You'll pass a rock quarry on your right, then another (lighted) tunnel with a sidewalk on both sides. About 2 kilometers long, it opens onto a harbor and a glimpse of nearby civilization. A slight uphill incline over rough road bends around and then down into **Malgrate**, a pretty lakeside town where we recommend getting lunch at the local pizzeria, café, or hotel. Lecco is a large industrial city, and we are going to route you the back way toward Como this afternoon.

At the junction just outside of Malgrate, which can be very busy, go right along the river.

At the roundabout take a sharp right (almost backwards) toward Como. The two-lane road rises and bends for several blocks. Chocolate lovers may enjoy an industrial-strength whiff of Lecco's chocolate factory from across the bridge. You'll go through the suburbs and a few lights as you wind along this busy thoroughfare for about 2 kilometers. A few sections of this afternoon's ride are less than scenic; we've done our best to route you to Como as easily as possible.

Take a right at the sign for Oggiono.

Follow the signs toward Oggiono. The road is flat and smooth, and the lake to your right placid and surrounded by marsh and meadow. A short upgrade curves around into a mountainous-feeling terrain and continues on a gentle upgrade into **Oggiono**.

   This small town skirts Lake Annone, sometimes called Lake Oggiono. You may want to make a quick stop to see the altarpiece and fresco in the church of S. Eufemia, which were created by Marco d'Oggiono, a pupil of Leonardo da Vinci.

Three and a half kilometers from Oggiono, turn right at the sign for Molteno. This section is a mix of agriculture and industry, but less traveled than the big roads.

At the roundabout, go right toward Molteno.

In **Molteno**, at the roundabout, go straight across toward the *centro*.

Follow the signs toward Centro.

Go left at the stop sign.

Across the railroad tracks after passing through town, go left at the sign toward Como.

Cross this busy street and follow the sign toward Erba. You ride along primarily flat agricultural land, where the lake appears to your right. Houses are more spread out here.

At the light, go right.

At the roundabout go right toward Como. You'll quickly come through **Erba**, a pleasing agricultural and industrial town in the Brianza hills. Although little remains of the medieval village, there is a romanesque church, an open-air theater, and nearby, the Buco del Piombo, a deep open cave, to visit if you have time.

At the roundabout with a light, go left on 639 toward Como.

Keep following the signs toward Como. A gradual upgrade moves through a more wooded area. You continue on a more moderate upward incline for over a mile, continuing to follow the signs toward Como. Follow the signs the remaining few miles into **Como**, and perhaps stay in another hotel that tempted you. The last 2 kilometers of downhill are sweet revenge for the climb out a couple of days ago.

DAILY SUMMARY

LAKE DISTRICT TOUR: DAY FIVE

Bellagio to Como

(50 kilometers; easy to moderate)

Note: Today's ride contains an unlighted tunnel. You should have
reflective patches on you and your bike. Also, bring a light.

- Follow the road left toward Lecco.
- Turn left toward Lecco after ½ kilometer.
- Turn right at the T fork toward Lecco after two blocks.
- In about ½ kilometer turn left toward Lecco and continue climbing.
- Follow the road left toward Lecco 11 kilometers from Bellagio.

- At the junction just out of Malgrate, about 18 kilometers, go right along the river.
- At the roundabout take a sharp right (almost backwards) toward Como.
- Take a right at the sign for Oggiono in 2 kilometers.
- Follow the signs toward Oggiono.
- Three and a half kilometers from Oggiono, turn right at the sign for Molteno.
- At the roundabout, go right toward Molteno.
- In Molteno, at the roundabout, go straight across toward the *centro*.
- Follow the signs toward Centro.
- Go left at the stop sign.
- Across the railroad tracks after passing through town, go left at the sign toward Como.
- Cross this busy street and follow the sign toward Erba.
- At the light, go right.
- At the roundabout go right toward Como.
- At the roundabout with a light in Erba, go left on 639 toward Como.
- Keep following the signs toward Como.

THE PIEDMONT
WINE COUNTRY

WHEN PEOPLE THINK OF PIEDMONT, THEY OFTEN THINK of the mountainous countryside to the north. Although this is a beautiful Alpine territory, we have not found it good for bicycle touring. The Alpine area is congested with cars and trucks—there's an *autostrada* right through the middle of it. It left us gasping for breath competing with the automobile pollution that settles in the Vallee d'Aosta. Therefore, we think you'll find the wine region of Piedmont much more satisfying to tour. It's quiet, much less traveled, and full of happy surprises for the cyclist. It's a gourmet region, so those of you who live to eat will find some good living here.

If you are a wine fancier, you will be in paradise. The Piedmont region is the Burgundy of Italy. The word *piedmont* means "foot of the mountain"—in French; the Italian word (*piemonte*) is seldom used. Here the grapevine is king. The area is home to such distinguished reds as Barbaresco and Dolcetto. The latter is not a sweet wine as the name would imply; only the grapes it comes from are sweet. One of the most famous names in bubbly wines, Asti Spumante, comes from this region, as well as hundreds of lesser-known wines. The area is rich in wine-tasting opportunities.

It is an agricultural area, where the *contadino* (peasant farmer) is greatly respected. Hazelnuts are grown in abundance here and figure prominently in many desserts. For some reason hazelnuts are not anywhere near as popular in North America as they are in Europe. Too bad. We love them, and look forward to Piedmont for the many delicacies containing this intriguing-tasting nut.

Alba is the white truffle capital of Italy. Should you pass through here in October you can take part in the annual truffle fair. We have never managed to land in Alba in time for this festival, but it is definitely on our agenda. Last time we were here we spent well over a hundred dollars on various truffle products to take back home with us, even though we had to carry them in our packs throughout the rest of Italy. Speaking of fungus, this area also is home to one of the world's premium types of mushroom, *porcini*. *Porcini* rank right up there with the *shiitake* in flavor. Eaten fresh on pizzas and in many other dishes, they have a hearty, rich flavor. If you like them you may want to pick up a batch of dried *porcini*, because they are a bargain in this area. In North America we have paid ten dollars an ounce for them; last time we were in Piedmont we bought several ounces for about eight dollars. The first night we were back home we broke out the truffle cream and our dried *porcini* and had a pasta feast to celebrate our return.

Another exotic dish that you will find nowhere else is called *bagna cauda*. An assortment of fresh vegetables will be served with a dipping sauce made of olive oil, anchovies, and an unconscionable amount of garlic. Bad for the social life, perhaps, but good for the taste buds. Around Alba we have seen a lot of people eating a local delicacy that does not appeal to us but may to you. It is called *carne cruda*, and consists of thin slices of raw meat with olive oil, lemon, and slices of cheese. After hazelnuts and *porcini*, the thing we most look forward to in Piedmont is called *bonet*. It is a dense, rich, chocolate pudding cake. It has a consistency all its own—a spoonful would tell you more than we could in a hundred words.

If you tour near Asti in June you may get to experience the festival called Festa dell'Agnellotto d'Asino. A celebration of the donkey, this festival is one of the few places where you can treat yourself to pasta stuffed with donkey meat. Although we were there for the occasion awhile back, we elected to forgo the pleasures of donkey-pasta. Even if donkeys are not your thing, you will find a great deal to stimulate your taste buds, and the rest of your senses, in this proud and gentle land.

DAY ONE: TORINO (TURIN) TO ALBA

(60 kilometers for the day; easy to moderate)
Our tour begins in Torino (Turin), and proceeds on the first day to the white truffle capital of Italy, Alba. Alba has a gentle sophistication and a very friendly, bustling quality that we hope you find as appealing as we did.

Torino is one of the larger cities in Italy, synonymous in many people's minds with the Fiat cars manufactured here. Your tour surprises start in this somewhat somber city visibly influenced by the French. If you go exploring you can find: the second-largest collection of Egyptian art and art objects in the world; prime examples of Baroque architecture; an ancient Roman bullfighting arena; a large palace; a large antiquities museum; and many fine piazzas, churches, galleries, other museums, and historical buildings. As with most cities in Italy, we found that it takes 18–20 kilometers to leave the city and get into the countryside. Be prepared for an hour of urban riding before you breathe fresh air.

GETTING TO TORINO

We begin this tour from the train station in Torino. It is very easy to get to Torino from anywhere in Italy. If you fly into Italy at Malpensa Airport near Milan, you can get a bus to the train station in Milan, then catch a train to Torino. There are many trains a day to Torino from Milan, including several expresses.

Head out the front of the train station and head to the right down corso Vittorio Emanuele II. You are in the heart of downtown Torino and will need to watch for streetcars and several lanes of traffic. You'll go eight blocks, past the Parco Valentino. The corso Vittorio Emanuele II is one of the main streets in Torino, lined with trees. Signs will say "Tutti le Direzioni."

After crossing the bridge, take the first right. You are crossing the wide Po River here.

Notice small signs directing you straight ahead toward Moncalieri. The overhanging trees are beautiful, and there is a bike path for several blocks.

At the next intersection follow the signs to Asti; basically go straight.

Do the same at the next intersection.

There is a small sign directing you straight ahead toward Moncalieri. This is a suburb of Torino with a combination of businesses and homes. After 3 kilometers you enter an area with more greenery, especially on the left. As you leave Torino proper, you'll see a sign: Moncalieri 2 k. The road is basically flat. Be careful not to turn onto the *autostrada* (marked in green).

At the stoplight, after a couple of blocks, go right toward Asti. This section has older homes and apartments.

At the stoplight 4½ kilometers from your start, go left.

Stay toward the left side, because you'll go left again at the next light (SS29). You'll go several blocks on this street (via

Cavour) through old stone buildings and small shops. A small town square is followed by a stoplight.

Stay on the main road through another stoplight. After several more blocks you'll see a sign indicating that Asti (SS29) is straight ahead. Be forewarned that you'll have a good 16 kilometers of urban sprawl heading out of the large city of Torino. The highway inclines slightly upward after 10 kilometers and narrows. You are still in the suburbs that service Torino.

Continue following the signs to Asti–Alba. You'll cross railroad tracks and then pass a sign indicating you've left Trofarello.

You'll go through a series of roundabouts here and hit some major traffic. Take the blue signs toward Asti–Alba until you have the opportunity to take the road straight across toward Poirino. You'll begin to see a little more greenery here with some agricultural land to the right. The road remains flat as you enter the outskirts of **Marocchi**. You come into **Poirino**, about 20 kilometers into your ride.

Go straight at the light and don't take the green arrows.

Go straight toward Alba at the fork.

Stay on the road toward Alba up a small hill lined by trees. You'll ride through flat agricultural land with wine advertisements and wildflowers dotting the countryside in season. Fine old farmhouses cluster off the road. A slight incline takes you up into **Pralormo**. You'll see your first rolling hills here.

Go right toward Carmagnola (sign: 14 k). You come into open farming country here with large granaries and long growing fields. The road is essentially flat.

Go left toward Ceresole d'Alba 2 kilometers after your last turn. This is, at last, a true bicycle road: small, untraveled, and rather bumpy, if level. Clusters of trees camp off to your right and occasionally line the road. A short hill winds around to your left.

Go straight toward the San Stefano. A growing orchard accompanies you and the road curves slightly downhill through **Berteri**.

If you're riding in late May or early June, you'll be treated to the eye-popping field of poppies on the left, with some rebels spilling over on the right. You'll say, "This is more like it," over the next few miles of gorgeous countryside.

At the next intersection go right toward (sign: San Grato and Fraz. Capelli). A moderate hill bends to the left and through a couple of switchbacks into a very narrow lane with orchards on either side. You'll crest the top after 2 kilometers and continue through lush orchards and vineyards. Another slight hill levels out, and you stay on this road. This area is as unpopulated as the first part of your ride was urban. A church and small trattoria mark the appearance of a little more civilization, and the view of the countryside expands on your right before you come into woodlands and orchards again. A patchwork of fields is visible below the trees to your right as you ride along the ridge. Small crests and dips take you beside farms and grapevines. The road turns downhill here, then you join the main road going left. You'll shortly enter **Monteu Roero**, where a spectacular view appears of the countryside for several kilometers. You then encounter a long downhill.

Stay on the main road downhill.

Shortly, go right toward Carneliano, Alba, and Bra. Leaving **Tri Nevi**, the road levels out with lovely wildflowers running riot through the corn. The surrounding hills are all cultivated with a variety of plants and vines.

Stay on the main road (_not_ to the right) at the next fork, toward Alba. The equipment for serious grape picking and processing lines this valley. Stay on the main road, following signs toward Alba. You are generally on a downhill course now.

After a couple of kilometers, go left toward Alba (sign: 9k). You come into **Corneliano d'Alba** and its mixture of old stone and new commerce. A narrow road leads the couple of blocks through this town and directly into **Piobesi d'Alba**. Many fields of poppies grace the hills here in season and compete with the growing commerce of the area. **Racca** appears next, easing you into civilization again at the next intersection.

Go right toward Alba. Mussotto, another small suburb, appears, and the road levels out.

At the light after a few blocks, follow the signs toward Alba.

Follow the signs to Alba Centro. You'll cross the Tianero River as you follow the signs to Centro.

Alba is a fine town to visit, even if you don't like truffles. If you do like truffles, however, which we are inclined to be passionate about, you will be in your element here. Many shops sell the prized delicacy, and if you happen to be touring here in the fall, you can get them fresh. The locals go out in hordes with their dogs, frequently staying out until midnight to find the elusive fungus. Alba is the home of the especially prized white truffle. Every June there is a mongrel dog fair nearby, because the locals consider mongrels the most skilled at sniffing out truffles.

Alba is the center of the Langhe (narrow hillcrests) region of Italy, which has its own rich history. Once dotted with forty towers, only thirteen now remain. Three of these are in the central piazza Risorgimento. Alba also has an interesting cathedral, several churches, and a museum of prehistoric and Roman artifacts.

The region is also known for its wines; you will have many wine-tasting opportunities as you cruise the back roads of this territory. Here also you will be surprised by the number of castles tucked in the lush woodlands of the region.

The tourist information center in Alba is a fount of infor-

mation about hotels, restaurants, and local sights. Located in
the center of town on via Vittorio Emanuele, they will load
you down with brochures that will guide you to all of the
vineyards, the over two hundred restaurants in the region,
and the castles of this area.

WHERE TO STAY AND DINE IN ALBA

There are several hotels right in central Alba that can give
you a comfortable night's stay. We stayed last time at the
Hotel Ave (via L. Einaudi 5, 12051 Alba; tel [0173]43933 or
42553). It's a very clean, reasonably priced hotel. Bicycles
may be parked in the courtyard, which is locked at night. Be
sure to request a room on the back side; otherwise you'll
likely be bothered by street noises. (Medium)

Another three-star recommendation is the Enomotel Il Con-
vento (cantina di Roddi 1, 12051 Alba; tel. [0173]615286),
which is out of the bustle of city center. (Medium)

The Hotel Savona is a big downtown hotel right around the
corner from the central plaza (via Roma 1, 12051 Alba; tel.
[0173]42381 or 30181). It is clean and convenient, although
somewhat impersonal. (Medium, high end)

One of the best restaurants in town is Da Beppe (corso
Coppino 20; tel. 43983; closed Tuesdays and in July). It's got
an extensive wine list, and you can get something with truffles
in it year-round. For the nontruffle-obsessed, they have a full
range of pasta dishes, roast meats, and some fish dishes. (Medium–Top)

Stella d'Oro turned out to be a really pleasant find for us (tel.
43921). We were in the mood for something quiet and quaint
that night, and this restaurant filled the bill perfectly. Toward
the end of the evening we were the only customers there, and
although the owners don't speak English, we had no trouble
ordering using our limited Italian combined with universal
sign language. The desserts were outstanding, including a

chocolate pudding that put us back in a good mood after a hard day in the saddle. (Medium)

DAILY SUMMARY

PIEDMONT WINE COUNTRY: DAY ONE

Torino to Alba

(60 kilometers; easy to moderate)

- Head out the front of the train station in Torino and head to the right down corso Vittorio Emanuele II.
- After crossing the bridge, take the first right.
- Notice small signs directing you straight ahead toward Moncalieri.
- At the next intersection follow the signs to Asti; basically go straight.
- Do the same at the next intersection.
- There is a small sign directing you straight ahead toward Moncalieri.
- At the stoplight after a couple of blocks, go right toward Asti.
- At the stoplight 4½ kilometers from your start, go left.
- Stay toward the left side, as you'll go left again at the next light (SS29).
- Stay on the main road through another stoplight.
- Continue following the signs to Asti–Alba.
- Continue following the signs toward Asti.
- You'll go through a series of roundabouts here and some major traffic. Take the blue signs toward Asti–Alba until you have the opportunity to take the road straight across toward Poirino.
- Go straight at the light in Poirino 20 kilometers from Torino and *don't* take the green arrows.
- Go straight toward Alba at the fork.
- Stay on the road toward Alba up a small hill lined by trees.
- Go right toward Carmagnola (sign: 14 k).
- Go left toward Ceresole d'Alba 2 kilometers after your last turn.
- Go straight toward the San Stefano.
- At the next intersection go right toward (sign: San Grato and Fraz. Capelli).

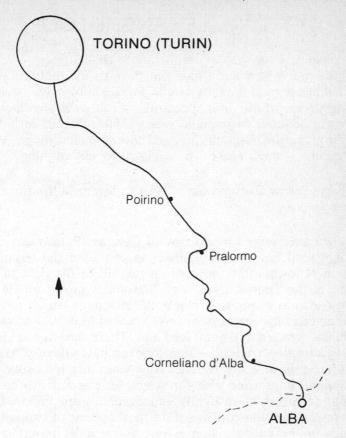

TORINO (TURIN)

Poirino

Pralormo

Corneliano d'Alba

ALBA

- Stay on the main road downhill in Monteu Roero.
- Shortly, go right toward Carneliano, Alba, and Bra.
- Stay on the main road (*not* to the right) at the next fork, toward Alba.
- After a couple of kilometers, go left toward Alba (sign: 9k).
- Go right toward Alba in Racca.
- At the light after a few blocks, follow the signs toward Alba.
- Follow the signs to Alba Centro.

DAY TWO: LE LANGHE LOOP

(70 kilometers for the day; moderate to challenging)
Today's tour will make a loop out through the foothills and
eroded hillcrests of the famous Langhe region of Italy, passing
through some of the most spectacular scenery the area has to
offer. In addition to splendid scenery, today's tour includes
wondrous castles, wine-tasting, and several quaint towns. We
will return at day's end to the comfortable city of Alba.

**To begin, follow the signs out of Alba to Savona in front of the
piazza Savona.**

Go right after several blocks toward Ceva and Bossolasco. The
straight road has a slight upgrade as you leave the business
section of town with vineyards up the hill to the right. The
grape of the famous local wine, Barolo, is grown on these
slopes. As you continue to climb, the incredible beauty of the
surrounding hills comes into view. You can look back toward
Alba and forward to the terraced hills. There is not a bad view
in any direction. After 5 kilometers you pass **Diano d'Alba**,
continuing up at a slight grade. Now vineyards are visible to
your right, intermixed with forest and little sections of corn.
The road curves more tightly and continues up. Follow the
sign toward Bossolasco. One of the most ancient and imposing
castles of the entire region is just a few miles past Diano
d'Alba. In Grinzane Cavour, the Castello Cavour is a thirteenth-century monument which was rebuilt in the seven-
teenth century. Former home to Camillo di Cavour, it is now
a wine museum that is open mornings and afternoons, except
on Tuesdays.

**You'll come to a fork at about 7 kilometers where one road
heads downhill. Be sure to stay on the high road here, following
the sign to Bossolasco.** You'll pass through an ancient tunnel,
and finally come to a downhill about 8 kilometers from Alba.
Orchards and vineyards line the hills as you stay on the main
road weaving down the hillside. The occasional stone farm-

house graces a ridge, and the lush roadside growth is regularly trimmed. You will see few cars on this pristine back road. Fog is not uncommon to this mountainous region, and certainly contributes to the magical, ethereal quality of the countryside. After about 11 kilometers the road heads uphill again through **Montefalco**. On the day we rode this leg, we were passed only by one car.

Follow the right fork toward Bossolasco, 13 kilometers out of Alba.

Continue following the signs toward Bossolasco. The vast valley on your right gives evidence of the abundance of this wine region. You are heading up, with some level areas in which to catch your breath. The grade is not steep, but it is continuous. The road is well maintained, and colorful wildflowers press the roadside. An endless series of orchards and vineyards accompany you, with the sweet smells of luxuriant growth. An occasional meadow appears as you continue following the signs to Bossolasco.

After 18 kilometers go right toward Ceva through a more developed town. You'll see a sign saying Bossolasco (9 k) shortly after turning. A more forested area follows this fork as you pass **Cavollotti**.

Take the left fork toward Ceva. You head upward again through another small village where more homes appear.

At the intersection go straight across toward Bossolasco. Lupins and poppies are joined by a wider range of wildflowers as the road levels out a little and becomes a bit rougher. Still snaking around the hills which drop off to the right, dense undergrowth clusters in the hollows, then opens into cultivation. Pastel houses with green shutters crowd the roadside, then become more scattered. As you traverse this ridge the road alternates between level and slightly uphill. Agriculture expands to include seasonal crops on the more level fields. The fine stone houses attest to the region's prosperity. Trees frame the road as you come into **Bossolasco**, your lunch stop after 28 kilometers.

Follow the signs to Centro. There is a *cremeria* and bakery that are open during the lunch break, but you may want to pack a picnic from the riches of Alba. The houses in Bossolasco have a more Swiss look. Poised between the Belbo and Rea rivers, Bossolasco is a much-visited Langhe town with an unusual main street. The shop signs here have been painted by local artists, and lend even more charm to this scenic town.

At the entrance of the town, go toward Dogliani and Somano. You actually head downhill here through the now familiar vineyards and forests. You may be happy to notice that the switchbacks are descending in elevation through fertile meadows and bushy forests. Three and a half kilometers after your lunch stop you pass **Somano**, continuing your downhill curves. Starker cliffs appear in the distance, as well as our favorite, wild blackberry bushes. Your first afternoon's slight uphill takes you through the *centro* before turning down again. Ancient and modern blend here, not unpleasantly, before you reenter a more lush woodland. The switchbacks are tightly wound here and the vegetation incredibly thick. Your biggest exertion will be using your brakes judiciously. The stone is tan and gray here, as you stay right on the main road. Another slight uphill rolls over into a beautiful little valley and **Dogliani**. As you traverse the largest town in the Monregalese Langa, you may want to stop and visit its well-known medieval section. And if time and inclination permit, you may also wish to sample its famous Dolcetto wine.

Turn right at the sign for Monforte, 10 kilometers from lunch. The roads here follow the layout of the hills and streams, giving your ride the pleasures of wild unhindered vegetation. The road is basically level for 4½ kilometers, then climbs a moderate hill between corn and wildflowers. The owners of the local vineyards have clustered homes on the hillsides opening to your left then right, as you climb on a slight incline into **Monforte d'Alba**.

In the center of this pretty town, turn right toward Roddino. You'll roll downhill past the fine old stone buildings of this health resort, then climb uphill for a short distance before leveling out past stone walls and more vine-covered hills. Another moderate climb winds along a somewhat bumpier road with alternating cultivated crops and vineyards.

Twenty-three kilometers after lunch, go left toward Seralunga (and a castle). A long and welcome downhill ribbons around the hills and crests the ridge. A sign lets you know you're in the region that cultivates the famous Barolo grapes. More sharp switchbacks descend through this fertile area, then rise briefly and course along another ridgetop. In the distance, one of the best castles in the area appears in **Seralunga**. The narrow lanes of this village house a wine-tasting site as well as the castle, which you will want to take time to explore. Known as one of the finest Piedmont castles, this thirteenth-century gem is open the usual hours and closed on Mondays. After this break continue on the main road. Big vineyards hug the steep hillside, but your route is level or downhill as you glide through **Baudana**. The tight switchbacks out of town descend into the next valley past larger wine-processing plants.

At this fork, you can take a left for 2 kilometers and visit another famous castle of the region, then rejoin the tour, which will turn right, going back to Alba from here. This valley road will proceed, gradually becoming more heavily trafficked. Just follow the signs back to Alba. You'll quickly encounter evidence of commerce in the outlying towns surrounding Alba. Industrial views are relieved at intervals with fields of poppies (in season) and some orchards. The road remains level, narrowing at times.

Go right at the roundabout toward corso Piave. The distant church steeple orients you toward the town center.

Follow the signs toward Centro.

DAILY SUMMARY

PIEDMONT WINE COUNTRY TOUR: DAY TWO

Le Langhe Loop

(70 kilometers; moderate to challenging)

- To begin, follow the signs out of Alba to Savona in front of the piazza Savona.
- Go right after several blocks toward Ceva and Bossolasco.
- You'll come to a fork at about 7 kilometers where one road heads downhill. Be sure to stay on the high road here, following the signs to Bossolasco.
- Follow the right fork toward Bossolasco, 13 kilometers out of Alba.
- Continue following the signs toward Bossolasco.
- After 18 kilometers go right toward Ceva through a more developed town.
- Take the left fork toward Ceva in Cavollotti.
- At this intersection go straight across toward Bossolasco.
- Follow the signs to Centro in Bossolasco after 28 kilometers.
- At the entrance of the town, go toward Dogliani and Somano.
- Turn right at the sign for Monforte, 10 kilometers after lunch.
- In the center of Monforte d'Alba after 4½ kilometers, turn right toward Roddino.

- Twenty-three kilometers from lunch, go left toward Seralunga (and a castle).
- At this fork in Baudana, you can take a left for 2 kilometers and visit another famous castle of the region, then rejoin the tour, which will go right and back to Alba from here.
- Go right at the roundabout toward corso Piave.
- Follow the signs toward Centro.

DAY THREE: ALBA TO ACQUI TERME

(62 kilometers for the day; moderate to challenging, with several strenuous hills in the morning)

Make sure to have a big breakfast in preparation for today's strenuous morning.

Leave town via the same exit as yesterday, opposite the fountain of the piazza Savona, heading toward Savona.

Past the commercial outskirts of town, go straight toward Savona (SS29). You come into suburbs and an area of small shops on this straight flat road. After 3 kilometers the road rises in a gradual incline, leveling for a block or two then rising again. Flower-bedecked balconies line the way.

After 6 kilometers take the left toward Savona. The slight upgrade takes you immediately into lush countryside, both cultivated and wild. The old homes mix red brick and stone with the traditional red tile roofs. The long, now moderate, uphill continues for several kilometers, with some switchbacks that speed your ascent out of the valley. The last part of your climb has some challenging sections, where it may be time to pull out the chocolate you've been stashing. Unremitting beauty on all sides tempers the strenuous nature of this ascent. After 13 kilometers of climbing you'll come to the next intersection.

Take the left fork toward Cortemilia and Savona. The town of

Benevello has one of the area's castles that you may want to visit before continuing. The road levels out across the ridge and begins descending past cultivated fields and stands of trees overlooking plunging valleys. After 16 kilometers you pass through **Borgomale**. Stay on the main road, which continues to descend quite steeply here, with old stone walls on the right guarding the drop-off into the forested valley. You'll enjoy the charming rustic villages along the route and the relative absence of car traffic.

In **Campetto**, continue on SS29 straight ahead toward Savona and Cortemilia. You begin climbing again through forested switchbacks on a moderate slope. Vegetation has overgrown the ancient walls in places, and fat irises winked at our efforts as we passed. Coming up out of this valley a long vista opens on your left over just the kind of terrain you're traversing. Three kilometers of climbing brings you into the old village of **Castino**. Capping the hill, this small village marks the leveling of the road, which then descends down the opposite side through more wine-growing regions. This is deep country, and the surrounding hills stretch out into the distance, interlaced with winding roads like this. This downhill is moderate, with some tight switchbacks at intervals. This strip is well kept and wide, although very lightly trafficked. At points the road is shaded by overarching trees.

Twenty-nine kilometers from Alba, take the left toward Acqui Terme and Vesime. You continue descending and follow the sign toward Acqui. The remainder of today's ride parallels the river, closely at times. The fertile valley is entirely cultivated and pocketed with stands of tall trees. You have some short small hills, but the road is basically level. Passing **Vesime** after about 5 kilometers, we recommend stopping for lunch at the corner restaurant.

Continue in the direction of Acqui. Your basic route here is to follow the signs to Acqui Terme. You have a little climb out of town, then a pastoral scene of river valley on the right and ancient buildings cresting the hills to your left. The nourishing river feeds the deep green and thick stands of trees, with the occasional small field of grapes. Large buildings dot the hill-side as the road ascends on a very slight upward slope to give you a higher view of the valley through the trees and bushes. You'll pass through **Bubbio** next, a graceful town of wrought-iron balconies and homes of stone. This moderately sized town may tempt you to stop and explore its church and center before heading downhill again toward Acqui. Some industry is situated here, and the river flows close to the road here for a short while.

As you take the left fork toward Acqui, another village, Monastera Bormida, disappears quickly. A short rise just out of town gives way to a hill-and-dale rhythm through the woods and fields. Private vegetable gardens look very productive, and after just a few kilometers you pass through **Bistagno**, a somewhat larger town whose main thoroughfare is lined with stately trees. You may be in time for a pleasant afternoon tea here before heading left over the railroad track toward Acqui. The green of the surrounding hills is refreshing and soothing, and the level road is comforting to the legs. As you approach Acqui the countryside is transformed into more populated and commercialized zones, although still with an overwhelming proportion of green.

Go left toward Centro and into Acqui Terme. Acqui Terme was a flourishing city even in Roman times. The Romans were quick to appreciate the pleasures of a good hot bath, and the thermal springs which give the town its name come boiling out of the ground from the Lake of Sorgenti and the springs of Acqua Marcia at 75°C. Poets and artists have celebrated the waters of this spa for centuries, and the historical sights of town attest to its long-standing political and commercial importance. Its eleventh-century cathedral has been renovated and contains a hall lined by columns and a beautiful Renaissance portal. More castle viewing is available here at the Castello dei Paleologhi, another restored eleventh-century site. Two large thermal springs operate in this city. The Nuove

Terme is open year-round, while the Antiche Terme is closed from October through April.

The tourist center is particularly friendly and helpful; the staff speaks English and will load you with well-produced brochures on every aspect of the region. They will also be happy to point you in whatever direction you want to go. Many people, believe it or not, come here to take mud baths, which are considered healing for sprains, strains, and contusions, as well as rheumatic diseases. If you can get yourself out of the mud long enough, you'll find plenty of other things to do in Acqui Terme, not the least of which is to eat. The truffle is king here, and you can have it flavoring your pasta as well as your meat dishes and fondues. There are some other regional dishes that are worth a try. You might enjoy a local sauce made of oil, garlic, and sardines, called the *bagna cauda*. In Acqui Terme we discovered the name of the chocolate pudding cake that had transported us elsewhere in the region; it's called *bunet* (or *bonet*). There are six wines here that have attained the distinction of being "of controlled origin." They are: the Barbera, the Cortese, the Brachetto, the Dolcetto of Acqui Terme, the Dolcetto of Ovada, and the Moscato.

WHERE TO STAY AND DINE IN ACQUI TERME

One of the best places to say is not actually in Acqui Terme, but just out of town. Reached by going across the bridge and turning left, then taking the first right up to the hotel, the Pineta (strada della Salita 1, 15022 Acqui Terme; tel. [0144]50688) is quite reasonable, comfortable, and much quieter than the in-town hotels. It has its own restaurant and bar if you don't feel like coming back into town for dinner. (Medium)

There are two fine hotels that house the thermal baths: the Antiche Terme (viale Donati, 15011 Acqui Terme; tel. [0144]52101), is a four-star establishment, with full facilities and a park. (Top) The Nuove Terme (piazza Italia 1, 15011 Acqui Terme; tel. [0144]50106) is also very well recommended. (Medium)

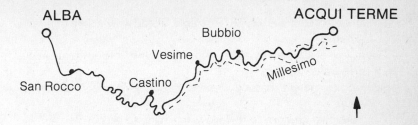

At last count there were twenty-five or thirty different restaurants, trattorias, and pizzerias in this rich gastronomic region. Of the restaurants that offer a complete menu, we can recommend three. Our first recommendation is La Schiavia (vicolo della Schiavia; tel. 55939); the other two are Parisio (via Cesare Battisti, tel. 57034) and Il Ciarlocco (via Don Boscol; tel. 57720). All of them have a wide selection of regional dishes and ambiance to spare. The Parisio specializes in wild game, mushrooms, and truffles.

In Italy, we frequently enjoyed a pizza and a salad in the evening. If this is your choice, you won't have any difficulty finding a good pizza or *panino* in this town.

DAILY SUMMARY

PIEDMONT WINE COUNTRY TOUR: DAY THREE

Alba to Acqui Terme

(62 kilometers; moderate to challenging, with several strenuous hills in the morning)

- Leave town via the same exit as yesterday, opposite the fountain of the piazza Savona, heading toward Savona.
- Past the commercial outskirts of town, go straight toward Savona (SS29).
- After 6 kilometers take the left toward Savona.

- Take the left fork toward Cortemilia and Savona 13 kilometers out of Alba.
- In Campetto continue on SS29 straight ahead toward Savona and Cortemilia.
- Twenty-nine kilometers from Alba, take the left toward Acqui Terme and Vesime.
- After 5 kilometers, passing Vesime, continue in the direction of Acqui.
- Your basic route here is to follow the signs to Acqui Terme.
- In Monastera Bormida take the left fork toward Acqui.
- Go left toward Centro and into Acqui Terme.

DAY FOUR: ACQUI TERME TO ASTI

(58 kilometers for the day; moderate)

Our destination on the last day of this tour is a town with a familiar name, Asti. In addition to its world-famous wine, Asti has a formidable military background, having once been dotted with over one hundred "tower houses." Asti is also famous for its jousting contests, said to be more ancient than those in Siena, and for its large number of festivals. You'll find many historical sites, churches, palaces, and museums in Asti, where we recommend staying an extra day to explore the environs.

Beginning at the monument in the piazza Italia, turn left at the top of via Monteverde. Follow the road around to the left onto corso Cavour, then right of corso Roma.

Turn left at the blue sign for Asti and take it out of town. Stay on the main road over the next few kilometers. You're back into countryside very quickly, with the railroad tracks on your right.

After 6½ kilometers, take the left fork (main road) toward Asti. You'll pass several old brick buildings and the Alice Bel Colle train station before turning uphill toward Nizza. The grade is slight to moderate, with some twists and switchbacks under the grand old wineries. The region here is more culti- vated, less wild, than yesterday's ride; every possible meter of soil is used.

Stay on the main road (to the left), which leads downhill through this agricultural heartland.

In **Castel Boglione** take the right fork, the main road, toward Asti. Several wine-tasting opportunities present themselves here before the road turns downhill and levels out with rich valley land to the left. About 20 kilometers takes you into **Nizza**.

There are several opportunities for lunch here, pizzerias and cafés. If you want the full treatment, try the Trattoria Savona (tel. 721573), where local specialities and mushroom dishes are offered. (Medium) This area was once known for the quality of its textiles. Now it is most famous for its wine, especially Bersano.

Continue following the blue signs toward Asti through town.

Right off the central square, turn right toward Mombercelli. This road quickly narrows into a lane past very pretty houses.

Continue right, uphill through these vineyards, then downhill after 3 kilometers.

Stay toward the left fork at the bottom of the hill (unmarked), as the lane threads through agricultural fields. This country lane is exquisite and basically untraveled. The roadside growth is regularly kept in check, giving you a clear view of this charm- ing valley.

Do *not* take the road toward Vinchio to the right. A slight uphill bends around tiny chapels and farmhouses, through or- chards and gardens.

At the T fork, go downhill to the right.

After another ¹/₂ kilometer, make a left up into the town of **Castelnuovo Calcea**.

At the T fork, turn left, downhill, toward Nizza.

At the bottom of the hill, turn right on the little road toward Cocito and Valmanella. The flat road parallels the railroad track and passes a lovely old willow as it leaves this rich valley land. You begin to climb again briefly and moderately out of the valley floor into your next intersection.

At the fork head right toward Montegrosso. The arching trees lead you through more shuttered homes lining the path into **La Generala**, then downhill around more lushly wooded hills into **Montegrosso**.

Go left at the stop sign toward Asti.

At the next stoplight, go right toward Montegrosso.

After just a block or so, take a hard right. Over your shoulder you'll see signs to Rocca. You climb moderately to steeply through town for about 1¹/₂ kilometers. This picturesque town has a fairly large church.

Take the right fork into town toward Moroni. You'll see a sign indicating the local feudal castle to your right. We recommend stopping to tour this picture-perfect sight before continuing to climb past homes with an enviable view of vineyards and hills.

At the fork, go left toward Rocca. The vistas are particularly striking to the left here, and the homes have luxurious gardens. The mix of wild and tended in this area is enlivening, an abundance of all forms of life that welcomes variety. Riding this high crest brings the periodic cluster of houses on neighboring hilltops into view. You turn downhill here, then up softly into **Santa Caterina**, another beautiful little village perched on this hill crest. The road (more like a lane) turns downhill and narrows before winding upward for a block or so. Up hill and down dale is the general proceeding for this section, through sometimes thick woodland. The homes are quite large, often of brick, and are tended with evident pride.

In the narrow lane through **Rocca d' Arazzo**, take your first left toward Asti. A 2-kilometer descent is followed by a rise lined with stubby round trees, then more slender ones as you climb through **Azzano d'Asti** on narrower lanes.

Take the right downhill toward Asti, with a red brick wall on your left. Another 2-kilometer descent through fields and vineyards comes to an L fork with the blue sign Asti pointing left.

At the next intersection in a couple of blocks, turn right toward Asti. You'll climb a small rise for a couple of blocks, cresting the hill and coming over into a cluster of buildings on the valley floor. A sign back over your shoulder indicates that you just passed through **Carretti**.

Follow the signs to Asti which head right. An especially fine red building nestles under trees as you come into the outskirts of Asti.

Go left, then right, up over the bridge into **Asti**. You'll have another 2 kilometers or so into the city center as you follow the Centro signs.

Asti is associated in many people's minds with the Spumante wine that flows abundantly in this region. The area also boasts a dozen other wines that have earned the "controlled" designation, including the popular Barbera d'Asti. This area has been a crossroads for thousands of years, even prior to Roman times; travelers have been staying in the inns and hotels of Asti since the middle ages. Perhaps this is why both hotels we have stayed at here found ways to overcharge us. One, which shall remain nameless, added surcharges that resulted in our paying over $60 for a short telephone call to the United States, while the other told us at check-in that breakfast was included, then charged us for it at checkout. Be forewarned in your negotiations here! Live and learn.

In addition to the fine scenery to ride through around Asti, there is a regional cuisine here that has made many a traveler hurry to arrive. If you happen to get here in the fall, you can join the throngs for the Seven Asti Gastronomy Days. They do a particularly good polenta in Asti, and they also specialize in meat dishes such as jugged hare.

WHERE TO STAY AND DINE IN ASTI

This is a surprisingly large city to ride into after your days of rustic riding, and if you elect to stay in one of the downtown hotels, you may be grateful that you packed your earplugs. On the edge of the city center is the Rainero Hotel (via Cavour 85, 14100 Asti; tel [0141]353866), a clean and pleasant hotel.

On the corner of one of the city piazzas is the four-star Reale (piazza Alfieri 6, 14100 Asti; tel. [0141]50240), which has its own highly regarded restaurant and is close to the city's fine shops and sights. (Top)

The smells of good food permeate the city center at dinner time, attesting to the dozens of food establishments for all tastes. The locals favor Ristorante Gener Neuv (lungo Tanaro 4; tel. 57270), on the shore of the Tanaro River, which serves a complete regional menu, including rabbit in wine and finanziera. (Moderate–Medium)

Also recommended are: Ristorante Falcon Vecchio (via San Secondo 8; tel. 53106) and Moro (tel. 32513). (both Moderate–Medium)

You may wish to do as we have and wander the little cobblestone lanes of the town center until the charm of a particular restaurant beckons you.

DAILY SUMMARY

PIEDMONT WINE COUNTRY TOUR: DAY FOUR

Acqui Terme to Asti

(58 kilometers; moderate)

- Beginning at the monument in the piazza Italia, turn left at the top of via Monteverde. Follow the road around to the left onto corso Cavour, then right of corso Roma.
- Turn left at the blue sign for Asti and take it out of town.
- After 6½ kilometers, take the left fork (main road) toward Asti.
- Stay on the main road (to the left) after 5 kilometers, which heads downhill through this agricultural heartland.
- In Castel Boglione take the right fork, the main road, toward Asti.
- Continue following the blue signs toward Asti, going through Nizza after 20 kilometers.
- Right off the central square, turn right toward Mombercelli.
- Continue right, uphill through these vineyards, then downhill after 3 kilometers.
- Stay toward the left fork at the bottom of the hill (unmarked), as the lane threads through agricultural fields.
- Do *not* take the road toward Vinchio to the right.
- At the T fork, go downhill to the right.
- After another ½ kilometer, make a left up into the town of Castelnuovo Calcea.
- At the T fork, turn left, downhill, toward Nizza.
- At the bottom of the hill, turn right on the little road toward Cocito and Valmanella.
- At the fork head right toward Montegrosso.
- Go left toward Asti at the stop sign in Montegrosso.
- At the next stoplight, go right toward Montegrosso.
- After just a block or so, take a hard right. Over your shoulder you'll see signs to Rocca.
- Take the right fork toward Moroni.
- At the fork, go left toward Rocca.
- In the narrow lane through Rocca d' Arazzo, take your first left toward Asti.

- After 2–3 kilometers take the right downhill toward Asti in Azzano d'Asti, with a red brick wall on your left.
- At the next intersection in a couple of blocks, turn right toward Asti.
- Follow the signs to Asti which head right after a couple of blocks.
- Go left, then right, up over the bridge into Asti.
- You'll have another 2 kilometers or so into the town center as you follow the Centro signs.

HILL TOWNS AND BACK ROADS OF TUSCANY

Introduction

OUR TOUR OF TUSCANY BEGINS IN FIRENZE (FLORENCE). Although we are not big fans of large cities, Florence is something special. The architecture, the amber light, and the friendly citizens all combine to make Florence one of the world's treasures. Outdoors, the city itself is a work of art. We remember standing on the piazzale Michelangiolo, a garden park overlooking Florence, and remarking on how the city is seamless. There is nothing to jangle the eye or disturb the flow. Indoors, of course, you will find some of the greatest art treasures on earth. The Uffizi Gallery contains countless masterpieces and has held centuries of art lovers in its thrall. Between the cathedral, museums, and piazzas, there is enough of what are considered the primary sights to keep you busy for days.

Florence is a great walker's city. Like London and Paris, Florence is built along a river, the Arno in this case. The Arno, which overflowed its banks in 1966, causing enormous damage, courses through the heart of the city. Florence is surprisingly easy to get around in. While we generally don't recommend riding bicycles in major cities, preferring to walk or take public transportation, it is possible to cycle around Florence. City maps are available everywhere and are very easy to follow. Florence is very tourist-friendly. There is a restaurant on nearly every block, and nearly everyone speaks some English. There are now even automated change machines where you can transform your dollars into crisp new lira.

Beyond Florence are the glories of Tuscany. Our tour steers you through such sanctuaries of the past as San Gimignano and Siena, where very little—and especially not the architecture—has changed over the hundreds of years since Leonardo and Michelangelo were here.

The food of Tuscany is glorious. In fact, if there is a better place to eat on earth we don't know of it. Not all food critics would agree, thinking the Tuscan fare to be too simple and severe. But the Tuscan table is perfect for the active cyclist. There is relatively little fat in this cuisine, and beans often replace the meats found in other areas of Italy. This is not to say you cannot get gourmet foods here. There are many fine restaurants that will serve exquisitely innovative dishes for a very steep price. But in Tuscany everyone eats well. Here, extra virgin olive oil—with its deep, rich fruity flavor—brings out the best of many dishes. We have often watched waiters bring a bowl of hearty Tuscan bean soup to the table, pausing to lace it liberally with olive oil. Since the terrible frost of the mid-1980s, which killed many olive trees in this region, olive oil is not the bargain it once was. In fact, we saw a bottle of our favorite brand on sale in Tuscany for more than we usually pay for it at our local fancy food shop. Still, it would be worth it at twice the price. Liver lovers must keep their eyes peeled for *fegatelli*, which is a shish kabob made from liver, bay leaves, and rough Tuscan bread. Speaking of bread, the Tuscans have raised the making of it to a high art. It usually comes in rounds, is unsalted, and need only be dribbled with a little olive oil or a smear of the local liver/anchovy paste to become a meal fit for a king. Tuscany also has a seacoast, which provides the region with fish such as mullet and cod. Be on the lookout also for *finocchio* (fennel) which in Tuscany is often baked with butter and Parmesan cheese and served as a side dish with meats.

Tuscany is home of the most famous of all Italian wines: Chianti. This robust red, often seen in its distinctive basket-bottomed bottle, graces many tables throughout the world. But there are also many lesser-known wines that have their passionate fans. We enjoyed the local wine of San Gimignano, finding it fruity and crisp. South of Siena is also home to the famous (and very expensive) Brunello, which some critics consider the best that Italy turns out.

We had been to other parts of Italy on other occasions, but it was not until we toured Tuscany that we felt that we knew what the country was really about. The Tuscans have a deep sense of who they are, and they communicate this feeling readily to the traveler

GETTING TO FLORENCE

Florence is easy to reach by train from just about anywhere in Italy. There are speedy trains from Rome, Milan, and Venice, as well as slower service that stops at smaller towns.

WHERE TO STAY AND DINE IN FLORENCE

In Florence we almost felt the need to redesign our price designations. As this is one of the most-frequented cities in Europe, hotels in recent years have responded by raising prices enough that our Low category doesn't exist in this area. We recommend staying in the hills northeast of Florence, in the picturesque and quieter town of Fiesole, whose views of Florence alone make it desirable.

From many of the rooms in the villa Aurora (piazza Mino 39, 50014 Fiesole; tel [055]59100), you can experience the kind of once-in-a-lifetime view over the valley into Florence that more than justifies the high price. Actually, by Florentine standards, the Aurora is in the low end of the range of Top. This small, comfortable hotel has old wooden doors, antique furniture, a well-trained staff, and newspapers in English (as well as other languages). Right on the town's central square, it is about ¼-mile walk to a wonderful country view and across from several restaurants and cafés. Also nearby are Fiesole's archaeological museum, which stores many treasures, and also the fine romanesque cathedral. (Top)

Just below Fiesole among wooded and gardened grounds is the Bencista (via Benedetto da Maiano 4; 50014 Fiesole; tel. [055]59163), a quaint old house turned into a pension. Half-board here with bathrooms down the hall is a bargain. (Medium)

If you feel the need to soak yourself twenty-four hours a day in Florentine ambiance, we recommend the Hotel Calzaiuoli (via Calzaiuoli, 6, 50100 Florence; tel. [055]212456). A four-star hotel enviably situated on the only pedestrian street of Florence, double rooms equipped with tile floors and modern fixtures can be reserved with breakfast. Each of its forty-four rooms has bath and telephone, and its location will provide a respite from big-city noise while remaining in the heart of Florence's main attractions. (Top)

One of the specialties of this area is a mouth-watering white bean soup with fresh garden and mountain herbs. Less well known but equally delicious is *fegatelli* à la Florentine, pork liver rolled in chopped fennel flowers, which is then stuffed into casings and cooked. And, of course, the term *Florentine* comes from here and connotes the use of a spinach sauce. Tuscans also do a mean antipasto, each restaurant specializing in certain dishes.

For good antipasti and pastas served by waiters who speak English and understand the international traveler, you will enjoy the Nandina, which is in the heart of the shopping district, on Borgo SS. Apotoli 64 (tel. [055]213024). We enjoyed the ambiance, with old wine bottles gathering dust on high shelves, as much as the excellent pasta and crepes Florentine. (Top)

Another beautifully decorated restaurant in the downtown area is the Cavallino (via della Farine, off the piazza della Signoria; tel. 215818), which has a very good-looking tagliatelle with porcini and a range of fresh fish, including salmon. (Medium)

Many people enjoy the international elegance of Harry's Bar (lungarno Vespucci 22 r; tel. 296700). Combining the moods of grand café and English pub, this restaurant, which is closed Sundays, has a wide menu. (Medium–Top)

There are dozens of restaurants, trattorias, cafés, and bars in Florence. The tourist information center can direct you to international or local cooking in a variety of price ranges and styles.

DAY ONE: FLORENCE TO MONTECATINI TERME

(61 kilometers for the day; moderate to challenging)

Today's ride will introduce you to the renowned characteristics of Tuscany: the brilliant quality of light, the rolling hills of gold and green, the sensuous rhythm of life here, and the delightful people who inhabit this magical land. After the relatively painless exit from Florence and its environs, you'll come immediately into some of the most glorious countryside in Italy.

Today's destination is the charming spa and resort town of Montecatini Terme, which has been restoring visitors for several centuries. We predict you'll be delighted by the holiday atmosphere, the lush grounds around the spas, and the exciting cultural tone of a town that knows and proudly shares its beauty.

Exit Florence on the west side toward Pistoia (blue sign also says Campi). You'll be on the via della Porte Nuove. Continue through the outlying area of Florence, following the signs toward Pistoia. Bear with us through this intricate set of instructions, intended to get you out of the city as quickly and aesthetically as possible.

Turn left, then immediately right toward Pistoia about 1½ kilometers after turning onto this street. Wind past the suburban part of Florence to a stoplight.

Turn left toward Pistoia onto a wider street.

Take the left fork after a couple of blocks toward Pistoia.

Continue following the signs toward Pistoia.

At the light, take a left then follow the signs up and around to the right toward Pistoia.

Take the right fork toward Pistoia.

At the light, turn left toward Signa, Pistoia. You'll pass a Chianti processing plant on your left as you come into a tree-lined section of the ride through residential and commercial areas. The road except for 2 blocks of elevation is flat and smooth. On Sunday, especially, you'll be accompanied by lots of Italians on bicycles. We were pleased to see a growing number of mountain bikes, our favorite mode of two-wheel transportation. There are no signs for several kilometers; just stay on the main road.

After 8 kilometers, take the road straight ahead toward Pistoia. Some countryside appears now, along with apartments and billboards. A slight rise takes you into **San Piero a Ponti**.

Go left toward Pistoia up over a bridge. Winding your way out of Florence continues on this pleasant road.

At the light after several blocks, go straight toward Pistoia and Poggio. A few grapevines crowd the road between buildings, as you stay on the main road, which is so far quite blissfully flat. You may wish to detour into Pistoia for a short visit before continuing toward Lucca, as Pistoia's central square is considered one of the finest in this area. The baptistry and cathedral in the piazza del Duomo are vividly decorated, while the two palaces, del Podesta and del Comune, are imposing in their grandeur.

After 16 kilometers, in Poggio, go left at the light in the center of town toward Carmignano.

After 2 blocks go straight at the light, then straight again toward Carmignano. The road begins to climb here. You can look back over your shoulder at the pretty village of Poggio. Now you are officially in Tuscan hill country, with olive trees and scarlet poppies lining the road. Your climb continues on a slight to moderate uphill into **La Serra**. The road levels out with the luminous light of Tuscany gracing the hillside. **Carmignano** appears right after La Serra, where houses cling to the hillside, and you climb a slight upgrade into the center of town.

In the town center go straight toward Vinci. Stay on the main road, which is lined with trees on the left as you begin to leave town. Climbing again, you'll see kilometers of hillside and the Arno valley in the distance. After a few kilometers you pass through **Santa Christina**.

Brief level areas are dominated by the preponderance of hills, now becoming moderate to steep, with switchbacks that quickly take you into the hills about 2 kilometers out of Carmignano.

This hill on the way to Vitolini is a real lung-buster and will reward your training for this tour. Some overhanging trees offer welcome shade from the bright Tuscan sun for which this area is famous. You may well want to stop at the pizzeria at the top of the hill to get a snack after your climb. Stay on the main road here, veering to your right and through deeper woodland. A downhill stretch opens out over the valley below, as the road ribbons past ancient walls and olive trees lining the hills. Five kilometers of downhill brings you into **Vitolini**, a gorgeous town of pastels and red tile roofs, where you take a small hill into town following the main road, and head downhill again as you leave town.

Just outside of town take a right toward the olive trees. *Don't* **go down toward Empoli, and** *don't* **take the hard right toward Faltognano. Take the middle path, which is unmarked.** This beautiful back road snakes down through terraced groves and meadows before leveling out along the ridge. A row of cypresses is outlined against the horizon, then the lane turns down again past vineyards and homes. You may see locals playing soccer at the neighborhood field. A sharp uphill brings you into **Vinci**, a delightful and good-sized town built, as are many other Tuscan towns, around a feudal castle. We recommend a lunch stop here. The Ristorante Gina is the quiet choice. An alternative you may also enjoy is the Torretta, which has a good view over rooftops and prides itself on its selection of local cuisine. The main square is lined with little cafés and stores, if you would like to eat more lightly.

You are dining in the birthplace of one of our heroes, Leonardo da Vinci. What were once a separate castle, library, and museum have been combined to form a center displaying the multifaceted genius of this local boy. You can visit except during the siesta time of noon to 3 P.M.

Your next move is a little tricky, as the road sign is on the side of the building after you turn. Basically:

Half a block from the town square, at the stoplight facing a small church, turn right going downhill. As you ride, you'll see the sign on the wall, Lamporecchio. The restaurant Gina is just ½ block away here on the left. Then the road climbs a short hill, descending into more cultivated vineyards. A series of hills progresses through the countryside past groves and wilder areas among the fields. A short 2 to 3 kilometers takes you into **Lamporecchio**, a large town with old and new buildings intermixed.

Just into town, take the one-way right, then turn left onto another one-way. You then go right toward Montecatini. You progress along the town's main road for several blocks.

Then take the left fork toward Montecatini. This residential area has a lovely tree-lined section through more populated areas.

Two kilometers after your last intersection, follow the signs to Montecatini around to the right at the fork.

After a couple of blocks go right again toward Montecatini. You'll pass through a series of small towns on your way into Montecatini, the first of which is **Castel Martini**. The road is fairly level.

Just outside of this town, turn right toward Montecatini. Farmland spreads out both directions as you pass through **Pazzere**. Small houses hug the road, which remains basically flat, with a few bumps over streams. Next comes **Monsummano**, where we saw a street named for John F. Kennedy across from one named for "M. Luther King."

Monsummano Terme follows directly, where you continue straight toward Montecatini. There is a story about this popular spa town dating from the last century. A local farmer was working his land and moved a large boulder, which revealed the entrance to a large cave threading back several hundred yards through calcified chambers into the mountain and ultimately to a lake amid the steam. Monsummano was instantly transformed from sleepy farming community to Monsummano Terme, visited and admired by the Grand Duke of Tuscany. Another transformation occurred in this century as Monsummano became a shoe manufacturing center.

Shortly after entering town, turn left toward Montecatini. The avenue enters a more commercialized zone here.

After several blocks take a hard left toward Montecatini (at a three-way intersection).

Follow the main road around to the right and notice the signs directing you straight ahead toward Montecatini.

After a few blocks, turn left at the stoplight toward Montecatini and Lucca. Coming up the main road a short hill brings you into the outskirts of town.

Continue following the signs toward **Montecatini**.

Take a right after a few blocks toward Centro. We noticed immediately that bicycles are for rent here, and a profusion of hotels greets your entrance into the town center.

Montecatini has been Italy's greatest spa for a long time. It has a wonderful feel to it. The air is sweet and fresh, the streets are clean, and there is a lively but relaxed ambiance throughout the town. The central area is perfectly suited to its main occupation: hanging out. There are endless opportunities for walking the shady lanes of Montecatini, and the surrounding hills provide beautiful opportunities for short rides. If you are hungry after today's ride, you can do what we do when we get to Montecatini—head for a world-class pastry shop, the *pasticceria* Giovannini, right in the center of town. It is usually swarming with gourmets drawn by its reputation, but well worth the wait.

Montecatini Terme has several spas, the three most famous of which cluster in the huge and lovely Paco delle Terme. The architecture in and around the spas is elaborately baroque and distinctly sumptuous. The tourist information center, for example, inhabits the corner store of the central promenade, and has large windows and a luxuriously appointed interior.

WHERE TO STAY AND DINE IN MONTECATINI

Close to the center of town is the Hotel Lago Maggiore (corso

Matteotti 70, 51016 Montecatini Terme; tel. [0572]70130). Rated at three stars by the government, the hotel has fifty rooms, all equipped with telephones and a comfortable, old-world feeling. It has a private garage where you can park your bike. (Medium)

If you are in the mood for a major splurge, you can do no better than the Grand Hotel e la Pace (via della Torretta, 15016 Montecatini Terme; tel. [0572]75801). This hotel has been catering to the rich and famous since 1870 and is predictably expensive. Rooms here start at about $200 a night and go considerably higher. But if you want to soak your tired legs in the same waters which have bubbled around Princess Grace and Sophia Loren, this is where to do it. (Top)

On the other end of the scale is the Biodi (viale IV Novembre 83, 15016 Montecatini Terme; tel. [0572]71341), on a quiet residential street. There is an indoor swimming pool, and a secure place to lock your bikes. (Medium)

Right down the street from the well-equipped tourist center is the Grand Hotel Nizza et Suisse (viale Verdi 72, 15016 Montecatini Terme; tel. [0572]79691). Close by the Excelsior Spa facilities, the Nizza's one hundred rooms all have telephone and private bath. You can add further luxuries as you wish, such as TV, bar, air-conditioning, and terraces overlooking the main avenue. A swimming pool and excellent dining room complete this hotel's possibilities. (Top)

Most of the hotels in this area, in spa tradition, rent their rooms with meals included. If you don't wish to do this, you will find many restaurants in town, including a large number with outdoor dining.

One highly regarded restaurant is the Gourmet (viale Amendola 6; tel. 771012). There is international cuisine here amid attractive Art Nouveau decor. The adventurous can try their rice dish with champagne and spider crab. (Top)

Another innovative restaurant is the Enoteca Giovanni (via

Garibaldi 25; tel. 71695), where the chef's creations include crepes with asparagus and rice with strawberries. (Medium)

WHAT TO SEE IN MONTECATINI

Montecatini boasts a grotto (the Grotta Maona cave with stalactite and stalagmite formations) and castle about 6 kilometers north of town. Across from the Hotel Nizza is the lovely Parco delle Terme and the fine old building of the Excelsior.

DAILY SUMMARY

TUSCANY TOUR: DAY ONE

Florence to Montecatini Terme

(61 kilometers; moderate to challenging)

- Exit Florence on the west side toward Pistoia (blue sign also says Campi). You'll be on the via della Porte Nuove.
- Turn left, then immediately right toward Pistoia about 1½ kilometers after turning onto this street. Wind past the suburban part of Florence to a stoplight.
- Turn left toward Pistoia onto a wider street.
- Take the left fork after a couple of blocks toward Pistoia.
- Continue following the signs toward Pistoia.
- At the light, take a left then follow the signs up and around to the right toward Pistoia.
- Take the right fork toward Pistoia.
- At the light, turn left toward Signa, Pistoia.
- After 8 kilometers, take the road straight ahead toward Pistoia.
- Go left toward Pistoia up over a bridge.
- At the light after several blocks, go straight toward Pistoia and Poggio.
- After 16 kilometers, in Poggio, go left at the light in the center of town toward Carmignano.
- After 2 blocks go straight at the light, then straight again toward Carmignano.

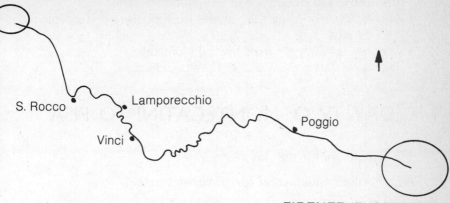

MONTECATINI TERME

S. Rocco

Lamporecchio

Vinci

Poggio

FIRENZE (FLORENCE)

- In the town center of Carmignano go straight toward Vinci.
- In 5 kilometers, just outside of Vitolino, take a right toward the olive trees. (*Don't* go down toward Empoli, and *don't* take the hard right toward Faltognano.) Take the middle path, which is unmarked.
- Your next move is a little tricky, as the road sign is on the side of the building after your turn. Basically: ½ block from the town square in Vinci, at the stoplight facing a small church, turn right going downhill. As you ride, you'll see the sign on the wall, Lamporecchio.
- Just into Lamporecchio (in 2–3 kilometers), take the one-way right, then turn left onto another one-way. You then go right toward Montecatini. (You progress along the town's main road for several blocks.)
- Then take the left fork toward Montecatini.
- Two kilometers after your last intersection, follow the signs to Montecatini around to the right at the fork.
- After a couple of blocks go right again toward Montecatini.
- Just outside of Castel Martini, turn right toward Montecatini.
- In Monsummano Terme continue straight toward Montecatini.
- Shortly after entering town, turn left toward Montecatini.
- After several blocks take a hard left toward Montecatini (at a three-way intersection).

- Follow the main road around to the right and notice the signs directing you straight ahead toward Montecatini.
- After a few blocks, turn left at the stoplight toward Montecatini and Lucca.
- Continue following the signs toward Montecatini.
- Take a right after a few blocks toward Centro.

DAY TWO: MONTECATINI TO PISA

(50 kilometers for the day; moderate)

Note: bring handkerchief for traversing tunnel

Our destination today is one of the world's most famous and recognized names, Pisa. Once one of the most important republics in the middle ages, Pisa has retained both its prominence and the beauty of the original monuments in the Campo dei Miracoli, which includes the Leaning Tower.

Along the way you'll lunch in the interesting and less crowded town of Lucca, which has several sites worth lingering over. The countryside today has both variety and the essential Tuscan features of sun and hills.

Exit town toward Lucca on via Anzanrio Sauro.

After 2 blocks, turn right toward Lucca (sign: 30k). You will be on via Ugo Bassi as you exit this extremely charming town. Trees line the avenue, then you pass under the train tracks and past the local stadium on a slight uphill.

Turn left toward Lucca at the stoplight.

Continue straight toward Lucca. Even the outlying buildings are festively designed with iron railings and tidy shutters. More trees shade you as the road bends and remains fairly flat, if somewhat bumpy.

Your basic direction this morning is *follow the signs to Lucca.*

Glancing to your right you'll see a pretty village up on the hill. Because of the distance of today's ride, we want to route you directly to Lucca and then Pisa, with time to explore these famous towns. Later in the tour we will be exclusively in small villages.

Go right after 7 kilometers toward Lucca. In **Fornacci**, shortly after your turn, you pass a short row of rustic brick buildings and small businesses. This road is relatively untraveled and leads quickly into **Pescia**, another picturesque Tuscan town. You may want to detour straight ahead to explore this cut flower center before turning left toward Lucca. A large stone arch marks the entrance to town, which is full of quaint buildings and shops. The whole town, which used to be known for making paper and tanning leather, is now surrounded by the colorful gardens which feed its flower industry.

Just 6 kilometers west of here, in Collodi, is the birthplace of Carlo Lorenzini's mother. Carlo who? The author of *Pinocchio*. A local museum commemorates the author and his puppet creations. Also in this immediate area is the Giardino Garzoni, considered by many one of the most beautiful gardens in Italy.

After turning you cross the bridge and turn left again, following the river for a short distance.

At the stoplight after ½ kilometer, go straight toward Lucca. You climb a short rise and pass a deeply shaded park to your right as you leave Pescia. The beautiful Tuscan hills rise in the distance, as does the road on a slight upward slope.

Continue following the signs to Lucca. Villas hide behind walls on the right, then the road descends into more rural land and **Lappato**, about 3 kilometers from Pescia. We could see why people are drawn to visit and live in this bright and serene area. You pass by Gragnono and an unusually large hotel for the countryside. The road turns up again, modestly, over a hill, then levels out and passes stone walls, manicured lawns and the occasional line of cypress.

Stay on the main road through Borganuova. With **Lunata**, you begin to enter the environs of Lucca. A series of small towns herald Lucca as you continue on this pleasant avenue on a level course into town. Stately residences and full trees line the road as you ride on more developed roads with more choices.

Take the road on the right toward the *centro.* Lucca is an ideal place to stop for lunch, which you will need to time for the noonish hours, as Lucca really shuts down during siesta time. This quiet medieval town doesn't appear to have changed much in centuries. For a long time Lucca was the de facto capital of Tuscany. It retains the former dignity of its eleventh- to thirteenth-century peak, even though nothing much happens here anymore. All of which is good news for the cyclist. Last time we were through here was on a Sunday, busiest day of the week for tourist visitation, and even some the streets of the old town were virtually deserted. We were heartened to see a group of a dozen or so senior citizens on a bicycle tour of the area.

The cathedral here was built in the eleventh century, although what is now visible to the eye comes from a renovation in the thirteenth. This striking building is a mixture of gothic and romanesque architecture. The two-color facade will show up again in other Tuscan towns. Inside you can view the famous tomb of IIaria del Carretto, by Jacopo della Quercia from the fifteenth century. There are several other churches worth seeing in Lucca, as well as elegant palaces and a national museum.

The famous red walls, which were turned into a beech and lime tree–lined ring surrounding the city in the 1800s, were the reason for Lucca becoming home to the International Center for the Study of City Walls. Believe it or not, there are international congresses and expositions on this subject. Remains of the earliest walls, dating back to Roman times, can be found in various parts of the old city. These walls once boasted towers and a moat. Most of the current walls were constructed in the sixteenth to mid-seventeenth centuries. The characteristic shape of the uneven polygon which forms these walls is quite different from the star-shaped fortifications built in the Renaissance. Besides serving as an effective fortress, the walls protected the city from the floods of the Serchio River in 1812.

There are many outdoor dining opportunities in the central part of the central city where lighter fare can be ordered. If you want something more elaborate for your midday meal, the Universo (tel. 43678) is perhaps the best of the fancier restaurants in the area just off the central plaza. For a full-course restaurant in our Medium range, you can also try the Buca di Sant'Antonio (via della Cervia 1–5; tel. 55881), which serves innovative cuisine in a fine rebuilt tavern.

Leave Lucca by the *senso unico* signs, heading back toward the walls of the old town.

At the light go straight toward Pisa (SS12). A large playing field walled in Lucca's renowned red brick continues for several blocks on your right.

Go left at this intersection, then left again after a block toward Pisa.

A quick right after only ½ block takes you up over the bridge and the train tracks. This wide avenue continues for several blocks.

At the roundabout head through and to the left toward Pisa.

After another block the signs to Pisa direct you to turn right. Stay on the main road, past gas stations and an old lumber mill, as you formally leave Lucca. The narrower passage is relatively level, and we were intrigued by a couple of restaurants and *pasticcerias* here.

Take the left fork toward Pisa. The tree-crowded hills roll off in the distance, and the eye is charmed by ancient churches, stone buildings and fields of grapes, corn, and vegetables. A gentle upslope reveals more sensational countryside. This grade continues for almost 3 kilometers before leveling out briefly.

We need to warn you about the tunnel you next encounter. The clouds of exhaust were visible. Put a handkerchief over your nose and go through as quickly as possible. On the other side is a delightful surprise: chalky cliffs and switchbacks descending to the valley floor. The narrow lane into Pisa here is lined by trees and surrounded by high banks and agricultural land. The tops of the churches become visible in the last few kilometers into town, and the rhythm of the shade trees as you pass is almost hypnotic. You enter the edge of **Pisa** in about 20 kilometers.

Turn left toward the town center.

At the T intersection, go right toward Centro, passing a block-long series of brick arches. As you come under a large brick arch you come into a section of storefronts.

Follow the riverfront, then cross the bridge going right at the light.

After you cross the bridge, go straight, where you will encounter a sign indicating Centro to your right. As you come into Pisa keep your head up and you will see the Leaning Tower. If you want to go right to the attraction, just point your bike in the direction of the cathedral dome and tower right next to it. Cars have to take a circuitous route to get to the attraction, but bicycles are not so limited and can take smaller streets and alleyways directly to the tower area. The top three attractions in town are grouped together in the piazza del Duomo, also colloquially known as the piazza dei Miracoli. The *duomo* (cathedral), the Leaning Tower and the baptistry are must-sees, although some visitors, including ourselves, are put off by the frantic tourist scene surrounding the attractions. Here you will see the largest number of plastic replicas of the Leaning Tower of Pisa gathered anywhere on earth. The tourist information center is located in the shadow of the Leaning Tower and is a helpful source of information about what to do and see in Pisa once you get past the main attractions. You can also pick up a useful town map to help guide you through the often confusing streets of Pisa.

The duomo here in Pisa is one of the most striking in Italy. Its facade is especially colorful and full of contrasts from the stripes of black and white stone, marble mosaics, and enameled glass. The Tower is known not only for its famous list but for the originality of its architecture. Unfortunately, you cannot currently climb its 294-step spiral staircase, but despite the tourist hype, you won't be disappointed at your view of the real thing.

In addition to the main sights, several museums, churches, and palaces are located in the Pisa area. This large and thriving city hosts a number of festivals and an opera season each year. You may also enjoy the nature park and the botanical gardens on the via L. Ghini.

WHERE TO STAY AND DINE IN PISA

Pisa is full of hotels and restaurants, not surprisingly, since some estimate that this town is Europe's number one tourist attraction. Here are three that we can recommend.

The Grand Hotel Duomo (via Santa Maria 94, 56100 Pisa; tel. [050]561894), is just a short ride from the Leaning Tower. It is a contemporary hotel with all the conveniences, including a locked garage where you can park your bike. (Top)

If you don't want to spend quite so much, the comfortable Royal Victoria Hotel (lungaro Pacinotti 12, 56100 Pisa; tel. [050]502130) is situated right by the Arno River. (Medium)

Also quite comfortable is the Hotel Arno (piazza della Republica 6, 56100 Pisa; tel. [050]542958), a small hotel with about thirty rooms. (Medium) These latter two hotels will put you halfway between the main attractions and the commercial center of town.

Most visitors of gastronomic bent and a healthy cash supply make a beeline for the Ristorante Sergio (lungarno Pacinotti

1; tel. 48245). The restaurant sits on the banks of the Arno in an old eleventh-century inn which has catered to the likes of Shelley and Montaigne. The price is high, but if your goal is to sample the full range of classic Tuscan cooking at one sitting, including fresh fish done in an original style, this is the place to come. (Top)

The locals favor Al Ristoro dei Vecchi Macelli (via Volturno 49; tel. 20424). It has one of the largest varieties of antipasti we've ever reported on, and their truffled cream sauce won its way to our hearts at the risk of hardening our arteries. (Medium–Top)

Pisa is also blessed with hundreds of small trattorias and pizzerias that offer more modest fare, including the Schiaccianoci (tel. 21024) and Pergoletta (tel. 23531).

DAILY SUMMARY

TUSCANY TOUR: DAY TWO

Montecatini to Pisa

(50 kilometers; moderate)

Note: bring handkerchief for traversing tunnel

- Exit Montecatini Terme toward Lucca on via Anzanrio Sauro.
- After 2 blocks, turn right toward Lucca (sign: 30k).
- Turn left toward Lucca at the stoplight.
- Continue straight toward Lucca.
- Your basic direction this morning is *follow the signs to Lucca.*
- Go right after 7 kilometers toward Lucca.
- After turning, you cross the bridge in Pescia and turn left again, following the river for a short distance.
- At the stoplight after ½ kilometer, go straight toward Lucca.
- Continue following the signs to Lucca.
- Stay on the main road through Borganuova.
- Take the road on the right toward the *centro* of Lucca.
- Leave Lucca by the *senso univo* signs, heading back toward the walls of the old town.

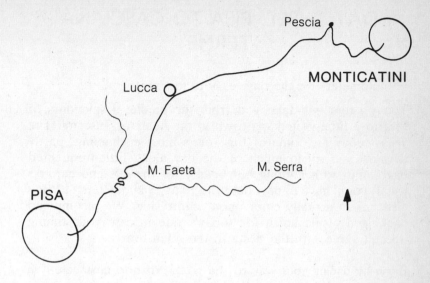

- At the light go straight toward Pisa (SS12).
- Go left at this intersection, then left again after a block toward Pisa.
- A quick right after only ½ block takes you up over the bridge and the train tracks.
- At the roundabout head through and to the left toward Pisa.
- After another block the signs to Pisa direct you to turn right.
- Take the left fork toward Pisa.
- Turn left toward the town center of Pisa after 20 kilometers.
- At the T intersection, go right toward Centro, passing a block-long series of brick arches.
- Follow the riverfront, then cross the bridge going right at the light.
- After you cross the bridge, go straight, where you will encounter a sign indicating Centro to your right.

DAY THREE: PISA TO CASCIANA TERME

(39 kilometers for the day; easy to moderate)

Today's tour will take you from the medieval splendors of Pisa to a little-visited spa town in the heart of Tuscany. The vistas today are some of this tour's most enchanting, partly because you spend much of the day along little-frequented back lanes with nothing but beauty for the eye and ear. As usual, you'll have to negotiate the 16 to 18 kilometers of Pisan environs to actually enter open countryside. We recommend packing a picnic lunch for today's ride in case your timing doesn't agree with the siesta in the small towns.

Begin by finding your way to the piazza Vittorio Emanuele II in the center of Pisa.

Go toward the arches of the station and its fountains.

Go straight through the first light after the piazza.

Turn left in front of the fountains. You are on the via Corridoni, on which you ride for a few blocks.

Take the left where indicated, then your first right.

After 2 blocks, at the roundabout, veer right on the one-way street.

Go left at the corner.

Go right on this main street, then another right toward Roma on the SS206. Your route through the suburbs of Pisa winds around tree-lined streets then comes parallel with the railroad tracks for a short distance.

After 6 kilometers, go straight toward Roma. This straight wide boulevard is not the most scenic, but our intention is to carry you out into the country most quickly. Fields of flowers and a sole willow mark the flat agricultural fields.

Go straight at the roundabout after 10 kilometers toward Roma. Up over an aqueduct and into more farming territory, the road continues to be level.

Stay on the main road straight through the next intersection. Passing over first a river then a major road, you come to an intersection.

Go right toward Roma at about 13 kilometers from Pisa.

Keep heading toward Roma through town.

After 16 kilometers, go left toward Colle Salvetti. You take a short hill up into town, a small, pleasant assortment of pastels.

Take the left fork toward Fauglia. Take the main road through town with occasional signs toward Fauglia. Here you can take a deep breath as you pass the long row of cypresses and enjoy what Tuscany is all about. The road, after the short climb through town, takes a sharp and winding downhill through thick trees and levels out in very green valley land. The fresh smells and sounds of birds announce **Fauglia**, where you have a short hill of about 1 kilometer into town.

In town go right toward Crespina. Be careful around this narrow corner, where you may want to stop and view the fine church before continuing on the one-lane road through Fauglia. This gem is what would be called quaint in any country, with several fine old buildings. Just as you leave town, pause by the wall and gaze at prime Tuscan vistas before reentering open countryside thick with vines and trees. Your downhill run levels out after a mile and proceeds through the rich shade of forest.

At the intersection 26 kilometers from Pisa, turn left toward Casciana Terme.

Go straight across in Laura, toward Casciana Terme. Hay bales may be stacked in the field when you pass, riding at first level, then on a gentle uphill grade, with a beautiful view of terraced green and buildings above you on the right.

Go left toward Casciana Terme. A gorgeous patchwork of textures and colors lines the hills. Your route drifts upward following the round hills, unpopulated but for clusters of sand and red-colored buildings on the far hills.

Rounding the hill, take the left fork 31 kilometers from Pisa. The road, now downhill for a kilometer or two, is rough in places. Turning up through open fields, the grade is slightly to moderately uphill for several kilometers.

At the top of the hill, take the left road toward Casciana Terme. Downhill again around sharper curves where we passed several local fruit stands, you quickly turn up again past vineyards.

Take the road on the right toward Casciana Terme. A more populated area appears on the left vista as you climb again into the loamy smells of forest.

At the fork after just 1 kilometer, go left toward Casciana Terme. Fine old trees accompany your final descent into **Casciana Terme**.

Follow the yellow sign left into the *Centro*.

This quiet little spa town is quite a treasure. While not containing any spectacular sights, the whole ambiance here is one of settled, soothing charm. We came to this town on a Sunday and were smitten with it. Not only do its hot baths offer a treat to the tired cyclist, but the central square is a perfect place to sit and sip while watching the locals promenade. On Sunday afternoon everybody brings their children out to the plaza. It is a day for gossiping and eating ice cream while children and grown-ups mingle. Here we found ourselves touched as we have been at other times in this country at the care and love the Italians express toward their children.

The countryside here is one of the main attractions. Everywhere the eye is greeted with rolling hills, which, if you came on a mountain bike, make for some dirt track excursions. Things move at a slower pace here in Casciana. Not much English is spoken here. The interaction with service people takes longer, but as a result, this area has a restful quality not found in the larger cities. It is also quite a bargain. Everything, the hotels, meals, the gorgeous fruits and vegetables, costs half what we had paid in Florence a few days before.

WHERE TO STAY AND DINE IN CASCIANA TERME

Our best recommendation is the Hotel La Speranza (via Cavour 42, 0587 Casciana Terme; tel. [0587]646215). Visible down a lane from the main square, this hotel has earned three stars, though it is still quite reasonable in price. We very much enjoyed sitting in the huge back gardens looking out over the hills behind the hotel. The bathroom was as large as the bedroom, and the large lobby has a very restful, comfortable feel. (Medium)

We can also recommend the very friendly Hotel Roma (via Roma 13, 0587 Casciana Terme; tel. [0587]646225), similarly priced. There is a very pretty enclosed courtyard, and the dining room here is very good. (Medium)

In our Modest range, Casciana Terme has a large number of pensions just off the main square.

As in many spa towns, the hotels expect their guests to dine on the premises. If you don't want to do this, make sure you let them know when you check in. We were in the mood for pizza the last time we were through here, and had two big ones at Il Caratello. You won't need reservations here. We had, in addition to our two pizzas, a carafe of white wine and a salad, all for the remarkably low price of about $16. There are other bars and trattorias in town, if you are simply looking for a sandwich to munch on or an ice cream cone to lick.

DAILY SUMMARY

TUSCANY TOUR: DAY THREE

PISA TO CASCIANA TERME

(39 kilometers; easy to moderate)

- Begin by finding your way to the piazza Vittorio Emanuele II in the center of Pisa.
- Go toward the arches of the station and its fountains.
- Go straight through the first light after the piazza.
- Turn left in front of the fountains onto via Corridoni.
- Take the left where indicated, then your first right.
- After 2 blocks, at the roundabout, veer right on the one-way street.
- Go left at the corner.
- Go right on this main street, then another right toward Roma on the SS206.
- After 6 kilometers, go straight toward Roma.
- Go straight at the roundabout after 10 kilometers toward Roma.
- Stay on the main road straight through the next intersection.
- Go right toward Roma at about 13 kilometers from Pisa.
- Keep heading toward Roma through town.
- After 16 kilometers, go left toward Colle Salvetti.
- Take the left fork toward Fauglia.
- In Fauglia, go right toward Crespina.
- At the intersection 26 kilometers from Pisa, turn left toward Casciana Terme.
- Go straight across in Laura, toward Casciana Terme.
- Go left toward Casciana Terme.
- Rounding the hill take the left fork 31 kilometers from Pisa.
- At the top of the hill after several kilometers, take the left road toward Casciana Terme.

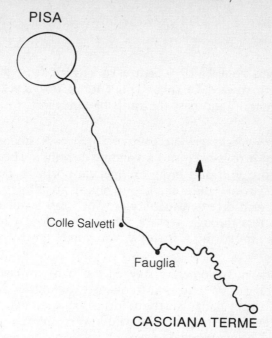

- Take the road on the right toward Casciana Terme.
- At the fork after just 1 kilometer, go left toward Casciana Terme.
- Follow the yellow sign left into the *Centro*.

DAY FOUR: CASCIANA TERME TO VOLTERRA

(50 kilometers for the day; challenging)

Today's journey will take you through some of the most beautiful back country in Tuscany. Pack a picnic because there are relatively sparse dining opportunities awaiting you. The destination today is the striking medieval hill town of Volterra, which is located so high between the valleys of Cecina and Era that it is called "city of the wind." Be forewarned that *you* may be winded after the final challenging climb into this fortress.

Exit Casciana from the large central parking lot. Go right following the sign toward Chianni. Uphill for a few blocks, you'll ride under trees and past the outlying vineyards.

After a few blocks go left toward Chianni. A steeper uphill greets you; it rolls over into a winding downhill. The Tuscany area is more arid and brighter than its northern neighbors. You can see how different geographical areas of Italy have produced such divergent life-styles. The road levels out after 2½ kilometers through very beautiful countryside. Following the ridges around the soft slope, you climb gently.

At the fork in 3 kilometers stay on the right toward Chianni. Still climbing, you'll pass infrequent farmhouses and more often the deep glades surrounding a local stream. Unusual birdsong and the fragrance of wildflowers increase the pleasure of this prime bicycling area. Olive trees compete with an undergrowth of more wildness in this area. As you round the hills, climbing, the vista expands to the far hills and the slopes of **Chianni**, one of the most beautiful little towns we saw in Italy. Continue on the main road through these stone and brick buildings hugging the hillside. A few kilometers out of town, the road finally turns downward into deeper countryside. Sometimes steeply with switchbacks, this rural lane descends into glades and over streams before climbing again at about 12 kilometers from your start. Traveling this road on a Monday morning in June, we were passed only by one car and by one well-muscled Italian cyclist. Rising at a moderate to challenging grade, the road ribbons through field and tree shade.

Turn left after 14 kilometers toward La Sterza. The downhill run here streams past farms and woods where the smell of blossoms is intoxicating. About 3 kilometers farther along, you level out briefly, then plunge again over a rocky stream, and then descend more mildly on the rough road through countryside with no houses in sight.

Four kilometers from your last turn, go left toward La Sterza. Fairly level valley land rolls on past random poppies and hills dense with bushy trees. A few fields of grapes bake in the sun as the road remains level. Some cypresses stand at attention as more cultivation appears, then more marks of civilization, such as a pottery store.

At the intersection after a total of 25 kilometers, go right toward Volterra.

Continue on the road toward Volterra, straight ahead. The valley floor continues with cultivated low hills rising to the right. Rich, fertile farmland blends many shades of green, and the light plays magnificently on hills that look furry with growing grain.

After another 5 kilometers, go straight toward Saline di Volterra.

Continue toward Saline di Volterra after a short stretch. Horizontal road, with occasional slight rises, carries you on through this valley. Passing very infrequent old buildings and the more frequent sign Strada Deformata (bad road), you can watch the clouds play over the distant hills as you peacefully glide along.

Stay left at 36½ kilometers from Casciana toward Saline di Volterra. The road climbs a little here then curves down again. Golden green hills blend into the distance as you cross a wide stream and flatten out again through the valley. A slight upward incline over the next 2 kilometers takes you past more patchwork fields and low hills. We were just remarking how few animals we'd seen on this tour when a crowd of sheep grazing on the next hill caught our eyes.

At 42 kilometers, go left toward Volterra. After a couple of kilometers the road rises for a very short distance, with rolling hills as far as the eye can see. When you round this hill Volterra appears on top and the vista of red against gold and green is spectacular. The road climbs again, sometimes steeply, with the city always in view on the ridge. You may be tempted to say, "I'm riding up there!?" You are.

After another 4 kilometers go left toward Volterra. Continuing up(!) you'll stay to the right along its walled houses.

Take the left fork between stone monuments with the view of town walls above.

Though the climb to get to Volterra may have you moaning and groaning as it did us, the view from the ramparts of this medieval city made it all worthwhile. The Etruscans lived up here before Roman times, enjoying the magnificent vistas and the sunny skies of this spot which is built on eroded (and eroding) clay and sand. Volterra's unusually uniform architecture has an austere aspect that is contradicted by the sunny friendliness of the locals.

There are a surprising number of things to see and do in Volterra, especially if your tastes run to archaeology. There are ruins of a Roman amphitheater, which are in the process of excavation. In addition, there is an Etruscan museum here, closed on Sunday afternoons (as are most museums in Italy). It has a collection including over six hundred funeral urns, many of which have vivid Greek motifs and painted scenes from mythology. Alabaster is the carving medium of choice here, and many shops offer pieces. Volterra also holds the oldest medieval palace in Italy, the imposing Palazzo dei Priori. You can imagine the centuries of strategic and pleasurable views from its walls.

The city itself is thankfully closed to motor traffic, making it a lot of fun to go strolling in. Well geared to the visitor, with a large and helpful information center, Volterra's old city will nourish you in many ways. Cycling up the hill to Volterra is considered a good thing to do by Italian cyclists, so you will probably find lots of other bicycle types to talk to while you're in town.

WHERE TO STAY AND DINE IN VOLTERRA

Our favorite place to stay is the tiny L'Etrusca (via Porta all'Arco, 37–41, 56048 Volterra; tel. [0588]84073). It is right in the heart of the medieval pedestrian district and very close the the famous Etruscan gate. Although its exteriors are medieval, inside it is completely modern and very clean. Best of all, it's a great bargain. (Modest–Medium)

Another option just inside the ramparts is the Albergo Nazionale (via dei Marchesi 11, 56049 Volterra; tel. [0588]86284). It has a huge dining room, and some rooms (all with bath and telephone) come equipped with TV. (Medium)

If you are in an expansive mood, you can reserve a room in the former monastery, San Lino (via San Lino 26, 56048 Volterra; tel. [0588]85250). The forty rooms in the four-star hotel are clean and well-furnished, and the price is still reasonable. (Medium)

Most of the restaurants in town naturally feature traditional Tuscan cooking and especially unusual game such as hare and boar in unusual sauces.

One of the best places to sample this hearty fare is the Osteria dei Poeti (via Matteotti 55–57; tel. 86029). It's in the medieval section, and is worth a visit for the decor alone. The ceilings are held up with vaulted brick against vivid white, which goes so nicely with the beautiful cutlery and crystal and the slightly formal setting. (Medium–Top)

Casual but very good and in a quiet side street, is the Ristorante Laq Grotta (tel. 86430). It has a huge menu of Tuscan regional favorites, but also features a fixed price menu for about $15 per person for lunch, dinner being a little higher. The day we were there the fixed price menu first course consisted of a choice of four pasta dishes. The second course offered a choice of meats, and the meal included vegetables and a sweet to end. (Modest)

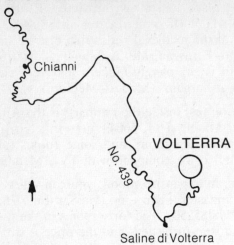

DAILY SUMMARY

TUSCANY TOUR: DAY FOUR

Casciana Terme to Volterra

(50 kilometers; challenging)

- Exit Casciana from the large central parking lot. Go right following the sign toward Chianni.
- After a few blocks go left toward Chianni.
- At the fork in 3 kilometers, stay on the right toward Chianni.
- Turn left after 14 kilometers toward La Sterza.
- Four kilometers from your last turn, go left toward La Sterza.
- At the intersection after a total of 25 kilometers, go right toward Volterra.
- Continue on the road toward Volterra, straight ahead.
- After another 5 kilometers, go straight toward Saline di Volterra.
- Continue toward Saline di Volterra after a short stretch.
- Stay left at 36½ kilometers from Casciana toward Saline di Volterra.

- At 42 kilometers, go left toward Volterra.
- After another 4 kilometers go left toward Volterra.
- Take the left fork between stone monuments with the view of town walls above.

DAY FIVE: VOLTERRA TO SAN GIMIGNANO

(30 kilometers for the day; moderate)

Today we move on to a town that is considered a rare treat by most people who come to visit. San Gimignano is one of Italy's hidden treasures, a place where the middle ages live on and will continue to do so for a long time. San Gimignano has been called the Manhattan of Tuscany because of the skyline provided by its remaining brick towers. At one time the town was dominated by upwards of seventy-five towers. Only thirteen remain now, still enough to give the town its dramatic exterior. Another impressive feature of San Gimignano is the mile-plus curtain wall that completely encloses the town, which hasn't changed appreciably since its apex of power in the fourteenth century.

Leave Volterra on the road toward Siena, then left toward Firenze. Even the outskirts of Volterra are extremely charming, with tan to golden stone walls and houses. Watch out for tour buses laboring up the hill that you're descending. There are some dramatically shaped hills to the left and patches of trees across the kilometers of surrounding hills.

Stay on the main road straight ahead. Climbing again along the hillside, continue on the main, twisting road (*don't* turn toward Mazola). The sharply defined hill to your left has a distinctive pattern of erosion on it, unusual for this area. After 1½ kilometers, the climb crests and descends around fertile hills, then climbs again on a moderate grade with more turns and curves. A pattern of hill and valleys meanders through this lovely pastoral-feeling countryside. The road is a little rough past some olive groves, which are followed roadside by thicker bushes (and insistent birdsong). After 10 kilometers, a steeper downhill rolls by trees planted for shade and the road then turns hill and dale again.

At the intersection after 11 kilometers, stay on the main road, which smooths out due to recent roadwork. Cresting the hill you may notice a strange structure on the hill resembling a hand with a pointing finger, next to a village.

Continue on the main road, which veers left. Your route becomes more coiled now, with views obscured by tall trees at times. Vineyards on the right and cypresses line the hill that courses upward. As you roll over the hill top you enter **Castel San Gimignano**.

Turn left just out of town. (sign: S. Gimignano) A gradual descent through flowering trees and fields with sheep takes you into some of the best countryside we've ever experienced. After 4–5 kilometers of descent you begin climbing the other side of the valley. Vines cover the trees, giving them an even thicker appearance. And if you are here in the early summer, the profusion of wildflowers is delicately entrancing. You'll pass, in this bright, pristine setting, something that is unmarked but looks suspiciously like a prison. The climb levels out after 4 kilometers and passes a great-looking stone trattoria (closed when we passed). As you round a curve at about 26 kilometers into the day you'll spot the famous "Manhattan" skyline of San Gimignano. Another downhill into cultivated fields may warn you about the climb up into town after a rest of 2 kilometers. The rise is slight to moderate, and you are surrounded by vineyards.

Take the left to **San Gimignano**. San Gimignano is a stroller's delight. Most of the medieval area of town is closed to all but foot traffic, so you don't have the annoying howl of motorcycles and horn honking that can disturb the tranquility of some Italian towns. There are not one but two tourist centers, the main one being right off the incredibly gorgeous central square, next to the church. Vines cover much of the ancient walls, cafés line the square, and the total mood proclaims sunny satisfaction. There is a municipal museum here as well as a museum of sacred art. The museum features pictures from the Sienese school and contains two acknowledged masterworks, a Lippi and a Pinturicchio.

San Gimignano is also a wine center. Wine enthusiasts will enjoy looking through the many wine shops for unique local varieties, and some of the vineyards in the vicinity offer free wine-tasting opportunities.

We found an unusual number of handicrafts shops in San Gimignano, from baskets and alabaster to wrought-iron work. You could spend hours just examining the range of boutiques along the cobblestoned streets.

If you visit during the season you will be treated by summer opera performances, concerts, and the occasional painting exhibition.

WHERE TO STAY AND DINE IN SAN GIMIGNANO

Just before you get to the town center there is a splendid hotel called the Relais Santa Chiara (via Matteotti 15, 53037 San Gimignano; tel. [0577]940701). One of the most pleasant places we've found in this part of Italy, this hotel is a quiet gem set on a promontory overlooking the vineyards and Tuscan hills. It is expensive and well worth it. With a heated, inviting swimming pool and forty elegantly appointed rooms, the hushed tranquility of this hotel is worth riding to. (Top)

Another real find in the heart of the medieval section of town is the Hotel Leon Bianco (piazza Cisterna, 53037 San Gimignano; tel. [0577]941294). The hotel is decorated in the rustic Tuscan style with vaulted brick rooms and has a lovely inner courtyard. It's also reasonably priced; you can even get a suite and still stay within our Medium range. (Medium)

If these two hotels are full, you might check out the Hotel La Cisterna (piazza della Cisterna 24, 53037 San Gimignano; tel. [5077] 940328), an ivy-covered hotel with a gorgeous,

SAN GIMIGNANO

VOLTERRA

No. 68

beamed dining room. The views from most of the rooms and the dining area are unbeatable. (Medium)

There are over twenty full restaurants and a large number of snack establishments in and around town. Two that we can recommend are the Ristorante Bel Soggiorno (tel. 940375) and Ristorante La Mandragola (tel. 940377). Both of these restaurants specialize in Tuscan cuisine and use the top quality local produce and cheeses in their cooking. (Medium)

While you're in the region be sure to try the Tuscan white bean dish called *vittelo*. San Gimignano also has more ice cream shops per square mile than any other place we saw in Italy. Many make their own flavors, and they try to outdo one other with both traditional and unusual flavors. One of our favorites was *crème caramel*; another was *nocciola* (made with hazelnuts).

DAILY SUMMARY

TUSCANY TOUR: DAY FIVE

Volterra to San Gimignano

(30 kilometers; moderate)

- Leave Volterra on the road toward Siena, then left toward Firenze.
- Stay on the main road straight ahead.
- At the intersection after 11 kilometers, stay on the main road, which smooths out due to recent roadwork.

- Continue on the main road, which veers left.
- Turn left just out of Castel San Gimignano toward San Gimignano.
- Take the left to San Gimignano.

DAY SIX: SAN GIMIGNANO TO SIENA

(52 kilometers for the day; moderate)

The final day of our Tuscan tour takes you to another medieval and magical city, Siena. This city was once the archenemy of Florence. Now the two rival each other as Tuscan beauty spots. The motto of the city says it all: "Cor magis tibi Siena pandit," which translates as "Siena opens its heart to you." Siena has been around since the early Roman era and has seen a vast and violent sweep of history unfold in and around it. After a tumultuous past, it evolved into an art center, which it remains today. The town itself is a work of art, from its central plaza—a masterpiece of harmony—to its graceful cathedral. It is altogether a fitting climax to a tour that began in Florence.

Leave San Gimignano by the road toward Siena, below the main entrance to town. You'll begin with a downhill where you'll want to watch for buses and trucks. Immediately coming into more pristine countryside, you will probably encounter more traffic in today's ride than on prior days. Beautiful old stone houses climb up the hillsides.

After 4 kilometers, take the road toward Poggibonsi. This flat road is surrounded by fields of wildflowers with tree-shrouded hills to both sides. A pretty little section of ancient trees provide early morning (depending on your starting time) shade. A more developed area follows, with wine-producing plants and a Ford dealership (the sacred and secular side by side, so to speak).

After 8 kilometers, go right toward Siena and Firenze.

Take another right after less than a block toward Poggibonsi.

In **Poggibonsi**, an important oil and wine center, first go straight, then right toward Siena and Firenze.

At the big intersection, go left toward Castellina. Continue straight on this central road for several blocks, in a town whose visual lack of charm is in sharp contrast to the potential of its name.

Go straight after a few blocks toward Castellina in Chianti.

Take an *immediate* right at the next block toward Castellina in Chianti. You shift uphill right after the turn. Although still in town, the environs soften and improve visually. After less than 1 kilometer you come into the outlying vineyards and the thickly forested surrounding countryside. The uphill turns more moderate and the landscape even more beautiful. Leveling out after about 2 kilometers you'll see sun-drenched homes capping the hillside overlooking the valley. Skirting this hilltop on another slight upgrade, the road smooths into more sinuous curves and comes into denser woodlands.

There are several beautiful, flower-bedecked homes along the hill crest interspersed with vineyards and the Melini Chianti processing plant. Originally developed by Laborel Melini, who invented the heat-treating process that allows longer stability and transportability, this impressive plant is now owned by a large conglomerate.

Bending into another slight upgrade, the even road enters dense forest with some pines. Occasionally the view opens to some rustic stone farm buildings as the mild upgrade continues for a few kilometers. Turning a little steeper after 3 kilometers or so, the road twists more tightly, and the vine-covered hills fall more sharply below. A celebration of sun and grape is in progress all around.

A vine-covered stone building signals the small Chianti producer's headquarters at the top of a rolling valley. The homes here look like the result of years of prosperity and are impeccably maintained.

The uphill enters more rural countryside again for the final climb into Castellina. Take a moment to look back across the valley out of which you've climbed. Several panoramic views are available in this next section, and the pines and cypresses march down the hillside in stately fashion. Stay on this main road through the various offshoots to either side.

Just before town are several signs to the right; *don't* take them. Continue into **Castellina in Chianti**, after 18 kilometers of steady uphill, for lunch.

Continue to the left, then a quick right, into the *centro*. A large supermarket is just inside the town center. Ristorante Latorre is near the tower, and Albergo Mariana is just beyond the pedestrian zone under some nice shade trees on the road out of town toward Siena.

Over lunch take some time to appreciate Castellina's important location and history. Pivotal in the wars between Florence and Siena, Castellina's unimpaired vistas, particularly from the top of the town's fortress, proved vital on many occasions. Situated between the Elsa, Arbia, and Pesa river valleys, Castellina ("small castle") is considered the most important of the Chianti towns.

After lunch, leave town toward Siena on the SS222. The view between the trees is outstanding, and you leave civilization behind after 2 kilometers or so. A hill leads out of town past some new developments (in the traditional pastel style). Leveling out, the road rises again over a short hill then rides the crest, giving you more excellent views. The basic direction for this afternoon is follow the signs to Siena. You'll see **Fonterutoli** just before you pass through it, after 5 kilometers. Now the road swoops downhill more seriously. Stone outcroppings jut out from the left, and the sun dapples through the lighter woodlands. Old rock walls mark the fields, where some well-tended roses draped the wall last time we came through. Vineyards compete with olive trees, and both are prospering. In the valley you'll pass a picturesque pizzeria and winery before ascending once again. You'll pass through **Quercegrossa**, huddling on this small hill, before the road flattens and passes more gorgeous stone homes. After a couple of kilometers you're in semirural environs again and have an opportunity to sample fresh olive oil at a roadside stand if you choose.

The road alternates between being level and having slight climbs as you enter the outlying sections of the city, heralded by signs for restaurants and hotels. As you round a corner at about 18 kilometers postlunch, you'll spot tall, modern buildings off to the left. Siena is a large city, and you are coming in from the north end.

Follow the blue signs toward Siena.

At the first stoplight of this afternoon's ride, turn left into Siena, and follow the Centro signs.

Siena is another one of those cities you'll be glad you rode a bike into. Car owners will find parking places here as scarce as midtown Manhattan. It's a medieval town with a modern city built around it. The main mode of transportation in vogue when this city was designed was the oxcart, and the millions of cars that descend on Siena during the tourist season are clearly alien to the sensibilities of this spot.

Many people think that Siena has maintained its character more than other medieval cities in Italy. It's a perfect place to end our tour. If you're in a hurry to move on, you can see the principal sights in a day, if you want to linger here for a while, you won't exhaust the pleasures of this city in a week.

The harmonious tone of Siena is only part of its fame. Extending over three rather steep hills, the walls of Siena have kept the medieval feel of Siena intact since the fourteenth century. The heart of Siena is the piazza del Campo, which many writers, including Montaigne, considered the finest plaza in the world. Even if cathedrals are not your favorite things to see, the one in Siena is worth making an exception. Dating from the twelfth century, with its incredible facade (a thirteenth-century addition), the colored bands of marble make this building unique. The interior is as richly detailed and exciting as the outside.

The town hall is another principal sight. This gothic building is thought by many to be among the finest public buildings in Italy. The information center, on viale Vittoria Veneto, is in sight of the Fortezza Medicea. Siena's fountains are also famous, the most impressive of which is the Branda fountain, which was built exclusively of brick in three leaping gothic arches between the eleventh and thirteenth centuries. Beautiful churches, streets, museums, and a monastery complete the official sights of Siena, although equal pleasure can be enjoyed by simply meandering through Siena's remarkably preserved streets.

WHERE TO STAY AND DINE IN SIENA

Last time we visited Siena we were on the last day of our Tuscan tour and felt like splurging. We pulled into the Grand Hotel Villa Patrizia, which you will see on your left just before you enter town (via Fiorentina 58, 53100 Siena; tel. [0577]50431). Lodging here is expensive; with dinner our tariff was about $250. It was worth it, though, because its quiet gardens and soothing old-world ambiance gave us a place to rest our weary bones and make the transition back into city life more gradually. Large tiled bathrooms come with thick terry-cloth towels, the staff is graciously helpful, and the breakfast brunch (included) could be the day's main meal. (Top)

In general, our recommendation is to stay a little out of town because of Siena's intense tourist scene. After the serenity of the last few days in the countryside, we found the tourist hordes in downtown Siena to be somewhat jangling. A lovely out-of-town alternative is the Villa Terraia (via dell'Ascarello 13; tel. [0577]221108). This villa lies on a hill about three kilometers from Siena. Its twenty-seven bedrooms are comfortable and clean. To get there, ride out via Simone Martini. After crossing viale Lippo Memmi, take a right on viale Sardegna and proceed until you get to via dell'Ascarello. (Medium)

The Garden Hotel (via Custoza 2, 53100 Siena; tel. [0577]47056) rests on a hill on the edge of Siena. It is not quite as expensive as Villa Patrizia, with breakfast included. There is a swimming pool and a restaurant where you can eat outdoors in good weather. (Top)

The locals consider Al Marsili (via del Castoro 3; tel. 47154) the best restaurant in the city. It is housed in the lower floors of the fifteenth-century Palazzo Marsili. A fine selection of antipasti will prepare you for some fairly innovative cookery. Here we found our favorite on the menu, those little potato dumplings called *gnocchi*. The well-stocked dessert tray is also a cyclist's dream. (Top)

You might also enjoy a visit to the Grotta Santa Caterina-da Bagoga (via della Galluzza 26; tel. 282208). If you're a truffle fan, you might try their beef dish cooked with these aromatic fungi. The chicken cooked in beer is also a local favorite. (Medium)

The Sienese area is known for its version of *panforte* (a spicy cake), delicious almond biscuits, and of course, olive oil. There is also a pizzeria and ice cream shop on just about every block, so your chances of going hungry in this town are happily remote.

DAILY SUMMARY

TUSCANY TOUR: DAY SIX

San Gimignano to Siena

(52 kilometers; moderate)

- Leave town by the road toward Siena, below the main entrance to town.
- After 4 kilometers, take the road toward Poggibonsi.
- After 8 kilometers, go right toward Siena and Firenze.

- Take another right after less than a block toward Poggibonsi.
- In Poggibonsi, first go straight, then right toward Siena and Firenze.
- At the big intersection, go left toward Castellina.
- Go straight after a few blocks toward Castellina in Chianti.
- Take an *immediate* right at the next block toward Castellina in Chianti.
- After 18 kilometers, just before Castellina in Chianti, there are several signs to the right; *don't* take them.
- Continue to the left, then a quick right, into the *Centro*.
- After lunch, leave town toward Siena on the SS222. This is your basic direction for the afternoon.
- Follow the blue signs toward Siena.
- At the first stoplight of this afternoon's ride, turn left into Siena, and follow the Centro signs.

UMBRIA: THE GREEN HEART OF ITALY

INTRODUCTION

UMBRIA OCCUPIES THE CENTER OF THE ITALIAN BOOT. IT is a land of valleys, rivers, and rolling hills. Everywhere there is green, green, and more green. This friendly region is home to fewer than a million people, so there seems to be more space here than in much of Italy. For those who thrive on viewing art, there are countless treasures tucked away in the cathedrals and museums of Umbria. For those who appreciate the relics of antiquity, there are several layers of civilization dating back to the Etruscan, followed by the Roman, medieval, and Renaissance. The National Museum of Archeology in Perugia is a must stop for students of Italy's history.

Umbria reached the peak of its power as a region in the late middle ages, from the middle of the thirteenth century to the middle of the fourteenth. As you tour the region you may marvel at how little anything has changed, except for the addition of cars and trucks. This detail has, on occasion, been a source of frustration for us as cyclists. It is sometimes hard to come out of the verdant countryside and enter a perfectly preserved medieval city, only to smell diesel fuel and hear the blaring of horns. If possible, we recommend timing your tour of Umbria so that you do it during the week rather than on the weekend. On the weekends the hill towns will be full of daytrippers from Rome and other big cities. You will be glad you came on a bike when you see the parking problems the motorists have to deal with in some of the hill towns.

This is the land of Saint Francis, whose hometown, Assisi, is still a major pilgrimage site for Roman Catholics. We never fully understood medieval religious fervor until we walked the ancient streets of Assisi. Umbria is the only place we have ever seen in Italy where there was a man at the door of certain cathedrals policing the attire of people entering the doors. He was on the lookout for people in shorts and women with sleeveless dresses. Monks, nuns, and priests are much more in evidence in Assisi than anyplace else we saw, except the Vatican itself.

There are no specific dishes that can be said to characterize Umbrian cuisine. Rather it is the manner of cooking that is distinctive. The wood-burning stove is still very much in use, as is the roasting spit. But everything is delicious here. To give you an example of what gives Umbrian chefs their pride, every year in Spello there is a feast honoring *bruschetta*, that wonderfully simple dish made of a crusty round of bread smeared with olive oil and garlic and toasted to a golden brown. Simplicity itself, but incredibly good. Umbrian chefs also take pride in unusual ways of cooking game and birds. Wild boar is frequently seen on menus here, as well as pigeons and small birds, some roasted whole.

The green-tinted olive oil of Umbria is considered by critics to be one of the two finest that Italy produces (the other being the oil of the Lake Garda area). The black truffle native to Spoleto's environs is also famous and used to flavor pasta dishes and omelets. Here, also, there appears a tradition that is not widely practiced farther north but is great for the cyclist: pizza by the slice. Look for shops that say "Pizza a Taglio." The farther south you go in Italy the easier it is to get this handy snack.

Wines are justly celebrated in Umbria. Perhaps the most famous are the golden wines of the region around Orvieto. Last time we were there we saw many cyclists stopping for wine-tasting in this area. The region around Perugia is also much visited by wine fanciers; we have heard people raving about the wine of Montefalco, particularly. We have not gone further in our wine exploration than ordering half-liters of the house white at various restaurants. It has been uniformly excellent, however.

The aspect of Umbria we have enjoyed more than anything else is the balance between the natural beauty of the land and the medieval towns that seem to grow so naturally from the land. Many times we have rested in late afternoon on the edge of an ancient town—our goal for the day—and looked back over the hills and valleys we had ridden through to get there. Most Umbrian towns are built on hills, so there is often an end-of-the-day challenge for the cyclist. There is a double satisfaction—the thrill (and relief) of accomplishment and the joy of the natural beauty—that brings a smile to the face.

GETTING TO SIENA

We begin in Siena, a city which we describe in the previous tour. See the end of the Tuscan tour above for a description of what to do and where to stay and dine in the medieval environs of Siena. It makes a good jumping-off place for Umbria, lying in the borderland between Tuscany and its southern neighbor. It is also easy to get to by train. If you are not continuing from the Tuscan tour but coming from elsewhere, you will probably come to Siena by train. It is very simple to get to Siena from Florence, taking the local. There are also several trains each day from Rome (if you are in a hurry, inquire at the station for the fastest—some of them make lots of stops before arriving at Siena).

DAY ONE: SIENA TO CHIANCIANO TERME

(84 kilometers for the day; moderate to challenging)

Welcome to the gentle green and beautiful landscapes that will take us into Umbria. The rolling countryside looks as much like a painted fantasy as it does the real world. Out of the soft light of this dreamy wonderland medieval towns have emerged whose austere purity has not changed in hundreds of years. This land gave birth to mystics like Saint Francis and also spawned a rich artistic tradition that is still celebrated today.

The bicycle tour begins from the parking lot of the train station in Siena. Our suggestion is to rest up in Siena for a day, because the first day's journey is a fairly long one and is best begun early in the morning. Our first day's route is still technically in what is considered Tuscany, and will take us by nightfall to the borders of Umbria.

Take a left out of the train station toward Roma. (Just down the road will be signs to Perugia.)

Up the short hill, veer left toward Perugia. You are basically following the periphery of the city.

Go right on SS2 toward Roma.

At the next light turn left toward Roma. The old city is up past the high walls to your right, and you head on a peripheral downhill for a couple of blocks, then wind around and up, still circling the old city area.

Continue through the next intersection, which heads downhill and over a brick bridge, toward Roma. High tower walls rise on the right, and you climb again after a few blocks.

Go left at the T intersection toward Roma. These charming old lanes lined with brick buildings head downhill. For an urban landscape, these red brick walls are quite pleasant.

Head through the next intersection to the left, toward Roma. Fairly flat now, the road continues to wander toward the open country.

Go right at the next fork after 1 kilometer. Very pretty houses and cypresses escort your exit from town on flat and downhill roads. After almost 12 kilometers you pass through **Isola d'Arbia**.

Stay right toward Roma. A few short blocks takes you through this small town and into valley land. **Ponte a Tressa** follows immediately, a town of well-tended rose gardens in front of tan and red brick houses. **More di Cuna**, another town of equal charm, follows on its heels, as your route remains smooth and primarily level.

In Monteroni d'Arbia, stay straight through the first intersection, which takes you into town.

In the heart of town, after 18 kilometers, turn left toward Asciano. You come immediately into pastoral countryside (we noticed that each big city in Italy takes about 18–20 kilometers to really exit). Directly, you will notice stands of cypresses and softly rounded, golden hills flanked by forests. After 2 kilometers a gentle climb begins through kind-looking hills. The colors are heathery, reminiscent of parts of Scotland, as you crest this hill after 1½ kilometers.

After a lazy 1-kilometer descent, you turn upward again, more steeply this time, through thicker woodlands and open pastureland. A row of cypresses appears as you round a bend, then a view of the gray-green hills to the right. Leveling out after about 2½ kilometers, you'll ride the crest of this ridge (with another short climb) to round past a beautiful home with brick gates. After surveying the countryside from the crest for a mile or so, including a beautiful drop to water on the right, you climb again on a slight upgrade for about 1 kilometer.

At the top of this hill take the right fork toward Asciano. You're taking the high road here, which gives you magnificent views in every direction. The mottled colors of the buildings where tan stucco has eroded away to red brick are enchanting, and the hillsides have a velvety look, with bush and tree borders for some fields (reminding us of parts of southern England). After 1½ kilometers, the lane begins descending and rounding into the valley. Long fields of vegetables line the valley floor, nestling into low, tree-topped hills. Basically level now, the road meanders past scarlet poppies as you approach civilization. A short, red brick bridge ushers you into **Asciano**. You may want to stop for an early lunch here, as there are several restaurants and bars in the *Centro*. This rather barren land has been sheep-grazing territory for some time. Excavations demonstrate that both the Etruscans and the Romans lived here. There was another flurry of activity in the middle ages, with not much since. After lunch you can tour the Museum of Sacred Art, which holds several valuable paintings and pieces of sculpture, including a Nativity of the Virgin by the Master of the Osservanza. Asciano also houses an Etruscan museum (open on request) with a variety of artifacts.

Take the main road through town.

In the center of town, go right toward Cassia and Mt. Oliveto. The pleasant streets of this largish town parallel the valley floor. As we paused for an espresso here, we passed four middle-aged Italian women on a bicycle tour. You reenter open countryside with Asciano visible back in the distance. Leveling out after a couple of kilometers, the passage then rises again past deeply eroded green-covered hills.

Nine kilometers from your turn, go left toward San Giovanni d'Asso. When we were through here, the hillside was ablaze with poppies. Wonderful surprises lie around each bend of this back road: groves of deep green, a line of cypresses surrounding a rustic farmhouse, riots of poppies. After being flat for 3½ kilometers, the road turns downhill past more disciplined vineyards and into deep woodlands.

In **San Giovanni d'Asso**, take the left toward Montisi.

A fairly steep downhill leads to a left toward Montisi and Sinaluhga. You turn uphill again on a moderate incline past more gorgeous scenery and into open countryside. Cresting the short hill in less than 1 kilometer, you can view San Giovanni's red roofs back off to your left. A brick factory huddles under the hills, and farms roll off in every direction; the road is lined with a variety of wildflowers and tall grasses. The sweet smell of hay is predominant. Some vineyards appear from time to time, but pasture and forest dominate the vistas.

In **Montisi**, go right, toward Trequanda and Castelmuzio.

After a short, steep downhill, go right toward Castelmuzio. What we call a screaming downhill takes you into a fertile little valley, where, in reverse of Newton's law, what goes down must go up. The land ribbons rather steeply through switchbacks with a breathtaking view of Montisi across the valley. After about 2 kilometers of climbing through this little shortcut, you enter **Castelmuzio**. This very lovely, tiny town of intimately spaced houses and rooftops is followed by a slight ascent following the hillside up and through the valley, where there is a rich tapestry of terraced trees and cultivated fields. Rounding a corner, you'll see **Petroio**, a striking hilltop town, which you climb to pass through, staying on the main road. You enter another long uphill through incredibly beautiful deep forest, followed by stacks of ceramics outside a local factory (this area is known for its ceramics).

Turn right toward Montepulciano and Pienza at 29 kilometers since lunch. Woodlands line the road for less than 1 kilometer, then the road weaves up and down through slight hills and dales over farms and fields that appear quite prosperous. A more moderate uphill of about ¼ kilometer crests and pulses

along the hilltop in and out of trees where you can easily view
the surrounding countryside.

Stay right at this intersection, toward Montepulciano.

**Stay right at the next intersection on the main road, toward
Montepulciano.** Ancient buildings grace the soft hillsides at
points, and the smell of ripening grasses is intoxicating. Some
orchards stretch over the hills as you climb another moderate
to steep hill to the stop sign.

Turn left to Montepulciano. A smooth road with only slight
dips and rises stretches out through the hills, where small
billboards announce the approach of a major town. Rounding
the corner you'll see the buildings of Montepulciano on the
far hill. Fairly level road takes you the remaining few kilometers into **Montepulciano**.

    If you take a little detour here, you'll enter the strikingly
situated town of Montepulciano, which was founded fifteen
hundred years ago by lowlanders fleeing the barbarian inva-
sions. It occupies the top of a hill of volcanic rock and affords
a sweeping view of the surrounding hills and valleys. If you
are not aching to get to the spa town which is the destination
of today's tour, there is plenty to see inside the old city of
Montepulciano.

    Montepulciano was thriving in the fourteenth century but
owes much of its resplendent architecture to the developments
of the sixteenth-century Renaissance and the efforts of San-
gallo the Elder. You can stroll along under the vaults and
arches of the original street plans and visit several fine palaces
and a well-maintained cathedral. The inner town, with its central plaza lined with impressive palaces, has a peaceful, harmonious feeling.

    This town is renowned for its splendid wines, especially
the Nobile di Montepulciano, the first wine to be granted
D.O.C.G. recognition and Brunello's competitor.

**The right turn toward Chianciano Terme occurs before heading
up into Montepulciano.** You have a little over 7 kilometers to

Chianciano Terme. Beginning with a slightly uphill ride, you descend again after a little more than a mile. A deeply forested hill looms on the right, and homes and apartments cluster under it. As you cross a short bridge, **San Albino** is the small town you pass (where you might begin to encounter the distinctive spa smell of rotten eggs). As you leave San Albino you'll pass several inns and a villa where the needs of tourists seem well mapped out. The road remains level or downhill into town.

Go right at the intersection here, toward Chianciano Terme.

After a long day's journey, you will probably want to head straight over to one of the four springs for a meditative soak. This town is devoted to the thermal baths, completely oriented to taking care of tired tourists. Chianciano Terme has a huge public swimming pool, along with the largest tourist information center we've seen in Italy. There is not much else to do here, unless you happen to arrive on a night when a musical event is in progress. It is a very pleasant place, though, with an abundance of that quiet, old-world feeling that is so rare everywhere else.

The original town of Chianciano has transformed into the medieval quarter, Chianciano Vecchia, which has preserved the castle, palace, and fine buildings along the via Solferino.

WHERE TO STAY AND DINE IN CHIANCIANO TERME

When we were here last, we stopped in front of the tourist information center on the piazza Italia and counted the hotels on its board, numbering over seventy. There are many different hotels in every category. If you're splurging, it won't cost you very much, as this town is visited mostly by Italians. Even some of the four-star hotels in town are in our Medium range.

The Continentale, right on the main piazza Italia (piazza Italia 56, 53042 Chianciano Terme; tel. [0578]63272) has a locked garage, swimming pool, and an enviable location next to a great ice cream shop. (Medium)

One of the most luxurious hotels in town is the Grand Hotel

Garibaldi (viale della Libertà 492, 53042 Chianciano Terme; tel. [0578]64681), where every amenity is provided for water lovers. (Medium)

If you'd like something quieter with a lot of local color, the Hotel Astra would make a pleasant choice. This hotel is located on the road into town about ½ kilometer before the main square (viale Lombardia 39, 53042 Chianciano Terme; tel. [0578]63166). (Medium)

As is the case in many Italian spa towns, most of the visitors tend to dine in their hotel dining rooms. If you don't wish to do this, there are several pizzerias and trattorias in and around the central plaza. The Ristorante Casanova lives up to its name by luring you with a fine view from the veranda and regional specialities such as tortelloni with ricotta and nettles (strada della Vittoria 10; tel. 60449).

DAILY SUMMARY

UMBRIA TOUR: DAY ONE

Siena to Chianciano Terme

(84 kilometers; moderate to challenging)

- Take a left out of the train station in Siena toward Roma. (Just down the road will be signs to Perugia.)
- Up the short hill, veer left toward Perugia.
- Go right on SS2 toward Roma.
- At the next light turn left toward Roma.
- Continue through the next intersection, which heads downhill and over a brick bridge, toward Roma.
- Go left at the T intersection after a few blocks toward Roma.
- Head through the next intersection to the left, toward Roma.
- Go right at the next fork after 1 kilometer.
- After almost 12 kilometers, in Isola d'Arbia, stay right toward Roma.
- In Monteroni d'Arbia stay straight through the first intersection, which takes you into town.

- In the heart of town, after 18 kilometers, turn left toward Asciano.
- At the top of the hill after approximately 9 kilometers take the right fork toward Asciano.
- Take the main road through Asciano after a few more kilometers.
- In the *centro*, go right toward Casia and Mt. Oliveto.
- Nine kilometers from your turn, go left toward San Giovanni d'Asso.
- In San Giovanni d'Asso take the left toward Montisi.
- Take the left at the bottom of the steep downhill toward Montisi and Sinaluhga.
- In Montisi, go right, toward Trequanda and Castelmuzio.
- After a short, steep downhill, go right toward Castelmuzio.
- Turn right toward Montepulciano and Pienza at 29 kilometers after lunch.
- At the intersection after less than 2 kilometers stay right toward Montepulciano.
- Stay right at the next intersection on the main road, toward Montepulciano.
- Turn left to Montepulciano at the stop sign.

- The right turn toward Chianciano Terme occurs after several kilometers, before heading up into Montepulciano.
- You have about a little over 7 kilometers to Chianciano Terme.
- Go right at the intersection in San Albino, toward Chianciano Terme.

DAY TWO: CHIANCIANO TERME TO ORVIETO

(68 kilometers for the day; moderate to challenging)

Today the route brings you into a land that time has bypassed, leaving the quality of the scenery and buildings much as it was centuries ago. Our destination is the incredibly located town of Orvieto, which crowns a huge block of volcanic tufa that springs up in the middle of the Paglia Valley. Tufa is the remarkable soil that is malleable when wet and dries to rock hardness when exposed to air.

Exit Chianciano from in front of the piazza Italia, heading toward Firenze and Roma.

At the bottom of the hill, turn right following the sign to Chiusi. You'll continue several blocks, with more possible lodgings beckoning from each side of the road.

After just 2 kilometers, take the left fork toward Chiusi. As you ride downhill you may notice a wine-tasting opportunity on the right, then you'll come into a lush area of fields of hay and unusual trees. The fairly smooth road is mostly flat with a few hills and dales. At 6 kilometers out you have a moderate but very short climb past wonderfully picturesque houses. The outlying environs of Chiusi begin almost immediantly in the little suburb of **Querce al Pina**. Intriguing shops intermingle with auto dealerships in this motley array of environments.

Take the left fork uphill toward Chiusi 9½ kilometers from Chi-

anciano. You'll see some opportunities to shop for the famous local pottery as you turn downhill now or ride level.

Another short stretch of greenery falls away into the left fork toward Chiusi.

A short, light climb levels out as you go right toward Chiusi.

Go right in **Chiusi**, toward Perugia.

One of the most ancient towns in Italy, Chiusi was bustling in the seventh century B.C. Its might led its Etruscan soldiers to attack Rome (unsuccessfully). Almost nothing remains from this apex except the road system which the Romans adopted in the fourth century. You may wish to stop briefly and tour the many Etruscan tombs and artifacts at the museum and the elaborate network of tunnels under the city before continuing.

A fairly steep and winding downhill follows the hillside then straightens out.

At 14 kilometers, turn left toward Orvieto.

After just 2 blocks come up over the bridge and turn left toward Orvieto. This elevated road takes you over the railroad tracks, where you continue on the left fork toward Orvieto.

Go right at the fork after less than ½ kilometer toward Orvieto. A moderate climb brings you back into countryside and the distinctive stone building style of this area. More vineyards march trimly up the hill and sometimes disappear into deep forest shade as the road does. You then have a long 4-kilometer, moderate climb past wonderful scenery.

At the crest, take the fork toward Orvieto. After a level period of less than 1 kilometer, you have another short, moderate climb into **Città della Pieve**.

Detour into this charming town to take a lunch break at one of its several restaurants. Città della Pieve still retains much of the medieval walls and fourteenth-century fortress of

its rich past. If you come any day but Tuesday, you may lunch
at the Ristorante Barzanti (via Santa Lucia; tel. 298010), on
homemade spaghetti or other local specialities.

**Come back out and at the outskirts of town take the right fork
toward Orvieto.** A breathtaking view of the medieval row of
houses of this beautiful town opens out, plus a spectacular
view down the valley. We particularly noticed here the building style that frames lighter stone buildings with arches of
dark red brick.

Just outside of town, go straight, following the sign to Orvieto.
(This is your basic instruction today.) Straddling the crest of
the hill, the road rises again out of town.

Follow the right fork to Orvieto 48 kilometers from your start.
After a short level span, you climb again past olive trees for
½ kilometer, then the road flattens out again and you roll
downhill into gold-tipped fields and little stands of trees. Just
2 kilometers later a rise rolls around the sometimes steep
dropoffs. After about 1½ kilometers more, the road loops
through a little hollow and climbs another short hill. Densely
planted trees lead through **Monteleone**.

Go right here, toward Roma and Orvieto. Distant towns strad-
dle hills across the valley on both sides of the road, which
winds downward into dense woodland. Slightly to moderately
at times, this smooth road continues to drop down. Another
2 kilometers brings you through **San Lorenzo**, another pretty
little town with flowered window boxes. The way continues
to drop as you leave town, passing some lovely outlying estates. You pass quickly through **Colle Basso**, then more downhill passes through the wood-shuttered stone buildings of
Spiazzolino, and directly into **Santa Maria**. All these little
towns are maintained with pride and are the facades of completely terraced hills of grapes. In the flat of the valley, hugging the hills to the left, the road widens slightly and comes
through **Fabro Scalo**. Many fine firs line the road here.

You continue straight through town, following the sign to Orvieto. After your short, 3-kilometer stint in the valley, climbing begins again, rather steeply at first around a narrower coil of road. The mostly moderate grade ascends into woodland on switchbacks, with a magnificent view back into the valley and distant hills. Entering deep forest with rich, loamy smells, the road emerges into a rather wild orchard and working fields where you pass through **Ficulle**. The road crests here and turns downhill after a 4-kilometer climb. The scenery is unremittingly gorgeous. Rounding a couple of bends, you climb briefly through town and another great valley view. A steadier climb leaves town past some tiny brick buildings and areas of well-tended vineyards and orchards.

After 3 kilometers, at the crest of the hill, go right (downhill!) on the main road. A semi-screamer, this rolling downhill reveals a seemingly endless series of undulating vineyards and towns in the distance.

Stay straight after 2½ kilometers toward Orvieto. A very brief rise bumps over into a view of the next magnificent valley as the road stays fairly level across this hilltop. A slight downward incline may sneak up on you here, so watch your brakes as you roll around this wilder Umbrian back country. We saw very few cars on this road, and blissfully, no motorcycles. We also noticed a marked absence of trash or debris, in contrast to some of the more populated areas. The slight downhill turns moderately steep, with the occasional switchback and house. A few more miles takes you to **Bagno**, a tiny community on the hill. More downhill, more woodlands in the distance, and some sharp turns bring you down into the valley where the river becomes visible. A straight shot across the valley of fertile agricultural land leads into woodland and a climb at a steady moderate grade for less than 1 kilometer. We saw lots of poppies in the fields and thick vines decked out on the trees. After another downhill your destination becomes visible in the near distance.

   First coming through the outlying areas, you'll see Orvieto on the hill, with prominent, modern-looking military buildings that are some of the few modern structures on the hill.

We especially enjoy how the Italians plant avenues of trees in their towns, and the outskirts of Orvieto have some great examples. Level road carries you along to a right fork toward town. Passing under the busy highway, you enter **Orvieto**.

That town you saw perched up on the hill is actually Orvieto, and where you are now is in the flatland outskirts. Unfortunately, when we were last here, there was still only one way to get up there. If you have 4 or 5 kilometers left in your legs, we highly recommend that you stay in the old city up the hill. If, after this relatively long day, you don't have it in you, there are several good hotels in the flats, such as the three-star Hotel Europa (see below).

Orvieto, with its striking location a thousand and some feet above sea level, draws a great many visitors annually. If possible, time your visit so that you don't arrive on a weekend in high season, because Orvieto is the closest hill town to Rome, with the capital city only 75 miles away. This was an Etruscan fortress town before it became a Roman outpost. You'll see the mark of medieval Christianity the moment you step into the central plaza, which was probably the site of Etruscan and Roman forums.

The cathedral here has one of the wildest facades we've ever seen, so spectacular that Pope John XXIII said that on Judgment Day God would personally send some angels to bear the facade back to heaven. It features elaborate marble sculptures and vividly painted scenes from the Old Testament surrounded by shining gold leaf, all topped by a large circular stained-glass rose window. The cathedral has another unusual aspect. The bronze doors (also on the facade) are modern, the work of a famous sculptor named Emilio Greco. Art critics are sharply divided over the doors, some considering them outrageous and some convinced that they are striking original works. It's fun to sit in the plaza and watch the ever-changing play of sunlight on the facade.

There are quite a few other sights to see, including a famous well that one of the popes ordered constructed in the sixteenth century out of fear that a siege might cut off Orvieto's water supply. The museum across from the cathedral stores remains from regional Etruscan burial grounds. You can also tour a magnificent example of twelfth-century artistry with tufa in form of the the Palazzo del Popolo, complete with arcades, mullioned windows, and an exterior staircase.

Throughout the old city there are tiny lanes that are ideal for walking and exploration. You will undoubtedly notice that Umbrian pottery is the chief tourist attraction in the commercial zone. The wine of Orvieto is also famous and well represented at local shops. Pope Paul III was especially fond of it, and over the years Orvieto wine has surpassed all other Umbrian wines in quality and popularity.

WHERE TO STAY AND DINE IN ORVIETO

If you plan to stay in the old city on the hill, the best choice is probably the Maitani (via Maitani 5, 05018 Orvieto; tel [0763]42011). Literally around the corner from the cathedral plaza and its brilliant facade, this hotel has much to recommend it. Big comfortable beds, spacious rooms, and sparkling cleanliness are standard. Many of the rooms feature art by a renowned local artist named Valentini. Also, for the cyclist's exquisite pleasure, rooms here have the largest bathtubs we encountered, generous even for the longest legs. The hotel has a lovely rooftop terrace where you can enjoy the passing scene. Rooms here are high, and breakfast is extra. (Top)

The splurge recommendation is 3 miles south of Orvieto, the Hotel La Badia (05019 La Badia; tel [0763]90359). Before it became an inn, the building was a Benedictine abbey and later a monastery. There are only about twenty rooms, so if you think you want to stay in this extremely comfortable and memorable inn, be sure to write or call ahead. (Top)

A more modest hotel located on a quiet side street in the old city is the Grand Hotel Italia (via di Piazza del Popolo 13, 05018 Orvieto; tel [0763]42065). It has a rooftop garden and clean, simply furnished rooms. The wealth of local color comes at no extra charge. (Medium)

If your legs protest too much and request a stay in the flatlands, the Hotel Europa (via Gramsci 5, 05018 Orvieto; tel. [0763]90359) is a fine three-star establishment on the right fork just before the ascent to the old city. (Medium)

Orvieto is well stocked with restaurants serving sturdy Umbrian fare. At the Trattoria Estrusca (via Maitani 10; tel. 44016) we had noodles with fresh white truffle grated at the table, and the best minestrone in the history of human experience. We both agreed that if we lived in Orvieto, we would come back there several times a week just for the soup. The restaurant is quiet, with high vaulted ceilings and very gracious personnel. We were pleased to see a procession of regulars greeted as we dined. (Medium)

The Del l'Ancora also has a good local reputation (via di Piazza del Popolo 7–11; tel. 42766). One of their specialities is tripe, a great favorite of Roman cuisine, though our courage failed us, and we cannot personally report on its quality. (The customers who were ordering it looked happy.) The vine-covered courtyard gives the place a restful atmosphere. (Medium)

Those interested in a more exotic dining experience might head for the Grotte del Funaro (via Ripa di Serancia 41; tel. 43276). A former rope-making factory dug out of tufa, the Grotte specializes in pasta with fish sauce, wild boar, and piglet.

We found these restaurants just by wandering around and moving toward what appealed to us; you may find other great places we missed once you are settled in your hotel.

DAILY SUMMARY

UMBRIA TOUR: DAY TWO

Chianciano Terme to Orvieto

(68 kilometers; moderate to challenging)

- Exit town from in front of the piazza Italia, heading toward Firenze and Roma.
- At the bottom of the hill, turn right following the sign to Chiusi.
- After just 2 kilometers, take the left fork toward Chiusi.
- Take the left fork uphill toward Chiusi at 9½ kilometers from Chianciano.
- Turn on the left fork toward Chiusi.
- Go right toward Chiusi after a short climb.
- Go right in Chiusi, toward Perugia.
- At 14 kilometers, turn left toward Orvieto.
- After just 2 blocks come up over the bridge and turn left toward Orvieto.
- Go right at the fork after less than ½ kilometer toward Orvieto.
- At the crest of the 4-kilometer climb, take the fork toward Orvieto.
- Detour into Città della Pieve after less than 1 kilometer to take a lunch break at one of the several restaurants.
- Come back out and at the outskirts of Città della Pieve, take the right fork toward Orvieto.
- Just out of town, go straight, following the sign to Orvieto. (This is the basic instruction for the rest of the day.)
- Follow the right fork to Orvieto, after 48 kilometers from your start.
- Go right after 2½ kilometers, in Monteleone, toward Roma and Orvieto.
- Continue straight through Fabro Scalo and toward the sign Orvieto.
- At the crest of the hill 3 kilometers out of Ficulle, go right (downhill!) on the main road.
- Stay straight after 2½ kilometers toward Orvieto.
- Passing under the busy highway, you enter Orvieto.

- If you are going to stay up in the old city, continue following the signs up the hill.

DAY THREE: ORVIETO TO TODI

(47 kilometers for the day; challenging)

Our shorter, but immensely scenic, route today ends in the interesting town of Todi, a mixture of styles, centuries, and artifacts. There are a few places to stop for lunch, but a greater selection of really wonderful picnic spots. So you pack some delicacies and head for the perfect shady knoll.

Starting out at the central plaza in front of the cathedral, take the only way out of town, down. If you elected to stay down in the flats, join us at the bottom of the hill.

Leaving town, the road takes you right, then to a fork.

Take the left fork toward Arezzo.

Go straight under the bridge (the way you first came into town).

After just a block or so, go right toward Prodo. This exceptionally smooth road launches immediately into the morning's first (but not last) uphill. Delightfully sweet smells waft around you on this moderate grade, which crests after 2 kilometers or so.

Take the main road toward Todi. A slighter uphill skirts a gorgeous stone house before leveling out across the fields and orchards of this splendid rural area. After a flat kilometer, a steeper climb provides some shade, welcome already if you are traveling in the summer.

The view improves (as hard as it is to believe) with this climb, which brings the now lower hill of Orvieto into sight across the valley. Thickly packed forests line the hills, and the homes you pass are vine covered and prosperous looking. The smell of hay adds a new note to the symphony of rich aromas as the road enters woodlands, still climbing. Some inviting flat rocks under pines may tempt you to rest a moment before continuing this challenging climb. A riotous field of cypresses, wildflowers, and bush looked as if someone had dumped the remainders of several seed batches in a hurry. More uniform green follows, and the slope lessens a bit, cresting into more open fields.

After 5 kilometers or so, **Collonetta** and its well-tended, beautiful homes appear.

Take the right fork here toward Todi. After leaving town the road descends into deep wild brush and woodland. Some vines compete for the forest floor before a rockier, more arid section of the road opens. You may exclaim as we did, "This is the life!" gliding through this unlimited vista of beauty.

A short, more level area of cultivation dips again into a steeper downhill, framed by tall trees and waving grasses. Some switchbacks will challenge your braking skill. Flattening out after 6½ kilometers, the road crosses an old stone bridge and begins climbing again. The sign **Prodo** appears and the road passes through the avenue of trees favored by Italians, for a short block. Still climbing, this moderate steady grade passes quickly into wildness again. Pause occasionally to look behind you as you round a bend where the view can be superb. Smooth meadows drop into scrubby brush at points as the road flattens out to a slighter grade, then climbs again to level out after 5½ kilometers. Poppy fields decorate the top, where we saw two cows, the first of the trip.

After 1½ kilometers of down or horizontal, you curve up again staying on the main road toward Todi. Flattening again briefly, the still-smooth road does a hill and dale interlude, where we saw a new foal and his mother enjoying the breeze. Up through fields with a sparser sprinkling of trees, the bright yellow of the road's shoulder contrasted brilliantly with the muted greens of grass and brush.

Coming level again after 3½ kilometers, the road presents a great vista before rolling into a short section of greater population and turning gently down. A fine little personal vineyard drank in the sun here. **Quadro** perches on the hillside here, a small village of stately stone homes and fields. The ribbon road still flings you downhill past an endless display of local beauty. More vineyards and patchwork fields dot the landscape, with villages visible in the distance. Another stone bridge leads into level road after 7 kilometers of moderate to steep downhill, then you whir downhill some more! Homes appear more frequently now, as you stay on the main road toward Todi. Cultivated fields extend as far as you can see. The curves straighten out somewhat as you continue descending.

Forty-four kilometers after your beginning, turn left on the larger road toward Todi.

After just a short distance, turn right over the river and toward Todi. Your last winding, 3-kilometer uphill of the day takes you up through vineyards and bush into **Todi**.

Continue following the signs into town—which involves yet more climbing.

Our top hotel recommendation is on your right before you get into the old medieval city. Be on the lookout for the Bramante, about which we will say more later. We recommend staying outside the city walls of the ancient part of town. Nothing has changed in this town since the middle ages, except for the addition of numberless cars every day during the tourist season, not to speak of scores of howling motorcycles. The streets are incredibly narrow and steep, and they are much better visited on foot than by bicycle. In other words, here is the place to put on your walking shoes.

The delights of Todi are just out of sight of the crowds that mill around the central plaza. Here, by walking the tiny back alleyways, you escape the hustle and bustle while getting a deep feeling for how life really was not too many years ago. Todi rewards the inquisitive with an authentic sense of a lost time. Along the back lanes one is likely to encounter an artisan at work at his trade or a pair of elderly ladies, heads bent in quiet and earnest gossip.

There were at one time over three hundred castles that defended the area, of which not very many are still standing. You can visit the best-preserved of them, Montenero, which sits on a hilltop not far from town.

According to one legend, the town of Todi was founded on the spot where an eagle deposited the cloth it had nipped from a prominent family's dinner table. Yet another legend has it that the town was founded by Hercules, although judging from the narrowness of the streets, we imagine that the town wouldn't have been big enough for him. Later in the town's history, the Romans came, bringing with them all the essentials of Roman life: baths, temples, and an amphitheater. In spite of the attractions of Todi, the town is somewhat overshadowed by the magnificent vistas of the Umbrian hillsides in all their glories. If you tire of the town itself, just walk over to the edge of the city and look out at all of Umbria spread below you.

WHERE TO STAY AND DINE IN TODI

The Bramante Hotel is, as we said, on the road coming into town (via Orvientana, 06059 Todi; tel. [075]8948381). A converted fourteenth-century convent, it clings to the hillside, affording many of the rooms a panoramic view of the famous vistas we've been extolling, including the river. Assigned four stars by the government regulating board, the Bramante is a pleasant-looking brick structure. (Medium–Top)

Two other hotels that would give you a comfortable night's lodging are the Hotel di Todi, which is out of town on the far side of Todi, on the turnoff toward Colvanenza (via Tiberina, 06058 Todi; tel. [075]8943646) and the Villaluisa (via A. Cortesi, 06059 Todi; tel. [075]8948571). (both Medium)

One advantage of Todi's location clinging to the hillside is that a lot of the restaurants have a good view of the valley. One such restaurant we can recommend is the Ristorante Cavour (corso Cavour 23; tel. 8942491). In a town of good pizzerias, cafés, and restaurants, this one is favored by many of the locals and is quite picturesque. (Low-Medium)

The Umbria (via San Bonaventura 13; tel. 882737) serves regional cuisine outside in the summer. Here you may find our favorite truffles on the pasta or dig into heartier venison with juniper berries. (Medium)

The dining room of the Bramante is also worth visiting, even if you're not staying there. Typical Umbrian fare is given four-star treatment here. (Top)

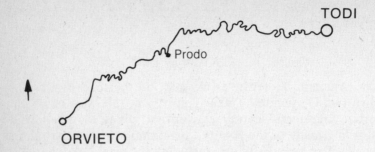

DAILY SUMMARY

UMBRIA TOUR: DAY THREE

Orvieto to Todi

(47 kilometers; challenging)

- Starting out at the central plaza in front of the cathedral, take the only way out of town, down. If you elected to stay down in the flats, join us at the bottom of the hill.
- Leaving town, the road takes you right, then to a fork.
- Take the left fork toward Arezzo.
- Go straight under the bridge (the way you first came into town).
- After just a block or so, go right toward Prodo.
- After 2 kilometers, take the main road toward Todi.
- After 5 kilometers go right in Collonetta, toward Todi.
- Forty-four kilometers after your beginning, turn left on this larger road toward Todi.
- After just a short distance, turn right over the river and toward Todi.
- Continue following the signs into town—which involves yet more climbing.

DAY FOUR: TODI TO SPOLETO

(55 kilometers for the day; moderate to challenging)

Today's travels span a wide variety of landscapes and moods, from deserted back roads to alpine smells and colors to sleepy resort towns. Your destination is the lively and successfully integrated town of Spoleto, where ancient history blends flawlessly with contemporary culture to create an atmosphere of culture-in-progress.

Exit Todi down a very steep hill where you should probably walk your bike to be safe. Follow the signs toward Terni, Perugia, and at the bottom of the hill, left toward Colvanenza and Foligno, as well. Circling the city walls, you'll turn right and head downhill.

Go right after 1³/₁₀ kilometers, toward Montenero. The downhill provides a magnificent view of Todi. This somewhat rougher road has many visual surprises, such as a cypress-enclosed estate next door to an auto repair shop. As you come down the hill, be sure to cross the railroad tracks, staying on the main road. The valley floor is rich with growth, vineyards, and a little grocery store. You climb up out of here after just a few blocks on a moderately steep, then less sharp upgrade. Wide open fields line the road, which tops out after just over 1 kilometer before rising again into **Vasciano**.

You'll get a chance to see the real agricultural center of Umbria today before heading into an art center frequented by the glitterati. The road dances up and down here, venturing into deep forest shade for a refreshing interlude, then crawling up a steeper hill and bypassing Montenero. This landscape is virtually untraveled by mechanized vehicles, which is one of its greatest charms. The up-down pattern continues.

After 15 kilometers, take the left fork toward Sismano. We suggest pausing occasionally to notice the surrounding hillsides, which are often topped with an architectural wonder.

A bit of a downhill screamer after 1½ kilometers should give you a start on the steep uphill that follows, for only less than 1 kilometer into **Sismano**.

A short, flat section flows past the intriguing walls of the old city and turns up past the "newer" homes and out into pasture and grassland. After a quick kilometer the road straightens and levels.

Go straight toward Montecastrilli. In **Dunarobba**, stay on the main road with its hiccups of short hills through this rather spread out town.

At the fork just outside of town, head right, toward Montecastrilli. Enchanting, rolling hills and the "Strada Deformata" sign let us know we were on a genuine Italian back road. And it's downhill past increasingly populated areas.

At the intersection 26 kilometers out of Todi, go straight toward Acquasparta. A gradual uphill comes into **Castelladino** after another 2½ kilometers.

Stay on the road toward Acquasparta: it goes straight then turns left after another block. It looks as if the outlying homes here are having a flower competition; the profusion of blooms is vivid. On a hill crest here the road is straight and flat for a while, allowing an unimpeded view of the Martani Mountains off to the right.

The remaining 4 kilometers or so into **Acquasparta** are level, pleasant agricultural land. In Acquasparta we suggest a large lunch in preparation for your more strenuous afternoon. There are a pizzeria, a couple of cafés, and a *gelateria* with pleasant outdoor tables. The main town road rounds downhill gently.

At the base of the hill turn right toward Roma.

Very shortly, after less than a block, turn left toward Spoleto. Passing under the highway, the wide road twists up at a steady grade, where you stay on the road toward Spoleto. From this angle, Acquasparta looks quite pretty. You're reentering high country again, and the cost is measured in uphills. You shouldn't encounter too much traffic on this road, however, which is wide enough to accommodate both two-wheel and four-wheel vehicles. The smells of deep forest tickle the nose, and the shade of the trees is quite refreshing.

The first afternoon climb is a challenging 5½ kilometers. After a few flatter turns and a brief rest, ascent continues. The grade is primarily moderate, although there are a few steeper sections. Long branches of trees look as if they're reaching out to touch you. On a day in mid-June, this road was virtually deserted. It probably won't be if you come in July or August or on a weekend.

After 8 kilometers a couple of stone buildings look very isolated out here, and the road turns over into a moderate downhill. You could be in the wilderness by the look of the land, but civilization huddles in the lower valleys. After 10½ kilometers the manifestations of civilization appear in full force in the form of the town of Firenzuola to the left, a gorgeous reservoir to the right, and rustic houses throughout. After a brief, semilevel section, the road snakes more tightly downhill past golden hilltops, cornrows of vegetation, and more glorious poppies. Although not edible like the friendly blackberries in France and England, these brilliant poppies provide nourishment for the soul. You'll continue on the road toward Spoleto, which shouldn't be difficult, as it's the only main road.

Flattening out somewhat again, there is a side road which you won't take. Cutting through the valley now, your passage is aided by sweet air that smells more alpine. Several small communities cluster off the main road, and there's more traffic moving at less than the usual Italian rate. After 18½ kilometers you roll through **San Giovanni di Baiano**, a gracious little village where you might stop for ice cream or other fuel. A modest level of population continues to be spread out along this valley thoroughfare. Someone seems always to be cutting grass somewhere, and your nostrils will register the delicious

odor. After about 4 kilometers of flat, the road rises slightly
and briefly, and you come into a more densely populated area
and **Spoleto**.

Here road becomes avenue and trees are more manicured. The town has a sun-drenched, lazy quality that rolled
over us and left us feeling deliciously indolent.

Spoleto is a special little place; Saint Francis was very
fond of its austere charm, and Gian Carlo Menotti gave it a
real boost when he chose the spot for his Festival of Two
Worlds. Now art lovers flood the town when the festival is
held, usually in June and July, to see plays, watch operas,
and listen to music.

Long before Spoleto became an art center, though, it
drew visitors throughout the millennia. Inside the cathedral is
a must-see work of art: a cycle of frescos by Filippo Lippi—
his last works. Legend has it that he was poisoned here as
part of a complicated medieval love vendetta. Lippi, in fact,
lived quite an exciting life for a friar. He eloped with a nun,
who later served as the model for the Madonna in some of
his paintings. Spoleto was in business before the Christian era.
If you have time, you can see the remains of a Roman theater
near the piazza della Libertà.

Spoleto is a great walker's town. Lock your bike at your
hotel, put on your walking shoes, and explore the lanes and
byways of this fine Umbrian town with its sweet air and sunny
skies. Early in the morning the fragrant piazza del Mercato is
worth a visit. It's where the flowers, fruits, and vegetables
are sold for the day's consumption. Americans can also feel
justifiable pride in the 60-something-foot-high statue that
graces the station square. It is by our own Alexander Calder.

WHERE TO STAY AND DINE IN SPOLETO

If you write well in advance, you might be able to get a room
in the unique Gattapone (via del Ponte 6, 06049 Spoleto; tel.
[0743]36147). It is a first-class hotel with a grand total of thirteen rooms in two magnificent buildings separated by a beautiful garden. It's hard to get to, situated up a tortuous road,
but once you get there you'll feel the satisfaction of an utterly

unique hotel. The views are splendid, and the level of service is very fine. It is only open in the high season, March–October. (Top)

Down near the center of town is a more modern hotel, very convenient and with excellent views. It's called the Hotel dei Duchi (viale Giacomo Matteotti 4, C.A.P. 06049 Spoleto; tel. [0743]44541). This hotel also has a reputable dining room. (Top)

One of the most colorful hotels (and we mean that quite literally) is the Hotel Aurora (via Appolinare 3, 06049 Spoleto; tel. [0743]223256). The interior is decorated in a decor that could be described as Early Vivid, with many candy stripes and odd juxtapositions of color. The staff are friendly, and the location is quaint in the extreme (a little courtyard). There is a safe place to lock your bike, and best of all, even with breakfast, it's very reasonable. (Medium)

One of the best places in town is the Il Tartufo (piazza Garibaldi 24; tel. 40236). For truffle fanciers like ourselves, it's like entering Valhalla. It had at least half a dozen different specialities that used the local black truffle. This luxurious establishment also has a tavern resting on a fourteenth-century floor. (Top)

Another pleasant restaurant near the Hotel Aurora is Il Pentagramma (tel. 47838). It has an intimate feel with lovely murals lining the dining room, and serves a variety of local specialities including their version of blackened mutton. (Medium)

Right on the piazza del Duomo, you'll locate Tric Trac da Giustino (tel. 44592) where you'll find many of the artistic types during the festival. When we were there last we were enjoying an espresso and beer outside before the dinner hour, and took many satisfying, deep sniffs of fresh vegetables and meats being prepared for the dinner meal. Gian Carlo Menotti's apartment is upstairs.

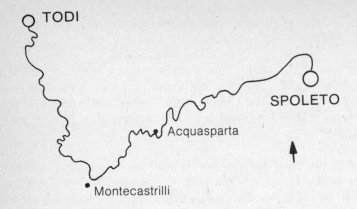

DAILY SUMMARY

UMBRIA TOUR: DAY FOUR

Todi to Spoleto

(55 kilometers; moderate to challenging)

- Exit Todi down a very steep hill where you should probably walk your bike to be safe. Follow the signs toward Terni, Perugia, and at the bottom of the hill, left toward Colvanenza and Foligno, as well.
- Go right after a bit more than 1 ³⁄₁₀ kilometers, toward Montenero.
- After 15 kilometers, take the left fork toward Sismano.
- After another 2½ kilometers, in Sismano, go straight toward Montecastrilli.
- At the fork just outside of Dunarobba, head right, toward Montecastrilli.
- At the intersection 26 kilometers out of Todi, go straight toward Acquasparta.
- In Castelladino, another 2½ kilometers, stay on the road toward Acquasparta, which goes straight then turns left after another block.
- At the base of the hill in Acquasparta turn right toward Roma.

- Very shortly, after less than a block, go left toward Spoleto.
- For the rest of the afternoon, follow the signs toward Spoleto, which is approximately 23 kilometers.

DAY FIVE: SPOLETO TO ASSISI

(64 kilometers for the day; moderate to challenging)

The grand finale of our Umbria tour is the mystical hill town of Assisi. The rampart-ringed town built in a fan shape of pink stone has probably not changed very much over the centuries since Saint Francis walked its streets. The saint known as a poet and a lover of nature became converted to the mystical path during a fever attack. Even if your health remains sound, you will likely be touched by the mystic soul of Assisi.

Most of the route today is fairly flat and smooth, with one major hill into the intriguing town of Montefalco. Before getting smug, though, remember that at day's end Assisi is 4 kilometers up from the valley floor.

Leave Spoleto going down the hill.

Take the right fork indicating Altre Direzione.

Go right toward Flaminia.

Follow the signs toward SS33 and Flaminia, and S. Giacomo at several junctions leading out of town.

Then take the main road toward Foligno. (We will take the main road for a few miles, then jump over onto smaller roads.) This wide boulevard leads straight and either horizontally or downhill out of the more populated area around Spoleto. There is a wide shoulder and lots of room for you and the relatively small number of cars you'll see. Businesses alternate with open fields, and an opportunity for *boccie* or boat-viewing appears as this main thoroughfare parallels the railroad tracks for a while.

Turn left in **San Giacomo** after 9 kilometers.

Follow the sign to Protte. This pleasant little lane rolls lazily through fertile valley land on a flat and fairly smooth surface.

In the small village of Protte (unmarked), at the T intersection, go right toward Camporoppolo. After less than 1 kilometer, go left toward Camporoppolo. Go through this small town on its level lanes lined by the rustic country homes.

Turn right after about 1 kilometer. When we were last here, either the sign to Bruna had been taken down, or it never existed. You're heading north (if you went straight across you'd be in San Brizio—just to locate yourself at this intersection). Still in the flatlands, this road cuts straight through growing fields of beans and other crops. After 3 kilometers or so you pass through **Bruna**, a small town dominated by the sixteenth-century sanctuary of Santa Maria della Bruna.

Take the left fork—the main road here—toward Montefalco. The mountains jut up way in the distance, and there is a castle visible to the left, a short distance off the road. The remains of the thirteenth-century Castel Riltaldi are well maintained.

At the fork right out of town, stay left on the main road. Even though it says Montefalco to the right, we prefer to take this back way, a more scenic route. A slight rise in elevation curves around these low hills of rich agricultural land. When we were last here it was just after the Giro d'Italia, and there were lots of bicyclists out flexing their muscles. A wonderful patchwork of small fields enchanted us.

At the top of this rise, turn right at the small sign to Montefalco—about 2½ kilometers after you began the short climb. Flat but somewhat rough road carries you past more aromatic agricultural fields and through a small farming community.

Just out of here, after 3½ kilometers, turn left toward Montefalco (the sign is a bit faded, or was, so watch for it). High, tufted fields of poppies and some cypresses in the road, which rises on a moderate grade and overlooks vineyards, orchards, and trees into the hollows. Warm sun and a wonderful quality of light give a glow to the land. After 32 kilometers this morning, we suggest stopping for lunch in **Montefalco**.

Follow the signs toward Centro in this fine old town. In the old city, as you first come into town, you'll see the Ristorante Falsico, and several *gelateria* and cafés.

This little town earns its name. It's perched like a falcon on top of the mountain. Here the panoramic views may nourish you as much as lunch. From this spot you can see almost all of Umbria on a clear day. Because of its strategic position, it's been destroyed at least once in its history, back in the thirteenth century.

After lunch, leave Montefalco toward Foligno. As you leave town you cross under an archway of trees and round down and around.

Continue right, toward Foligno. Stay on this beautiful main road as it twists down the colorful hillside, displaying a wealth of vegetative texture on surrounding hillsides. People have clearly been cherishing this land for centuries, and it glows with ripeness. Every inch is cultivated, and there is an interesting variety of plants and vines. On the valley floor, thick stands of grass abound and the road is wide and level.

Six kilometers after descending from Montefalco you'll see a little side road with two signs, Bar Calipso and Panini Vino. Take this road which veers off the main one to the left. Keep following this road as it first curves sharply to the left, then rounds along the valley with a short rise. This deserted back lane has the company of thick fields and parallels a canal closely at points.

At the junction 4½ kilometers after you venture into really back roads, turn right over the bridge, then straight toward Bevagna. Follow the signs through this lovely old city on the

piazzale Guelo. Flourishing during the Roman era, this ancient town retains its medieval walls, town center, and distinctly old-world flavor. Two stunning romanesque churches
are worth touring.

Go left toward Torre del Colle and Cannara.

**Just outside of the town, take an immediate right toward
Cannara.**

Keep following the signs toward Cannara. Passing through
Capro shortly, the valley floor is lush with trees and fields.
Rising over short hills and on a very slight grade, the road
then levels out and curves very gently along through this green
heartland of Umbria.

**Stay on the main road that bypasses Cantalupo, tracing an erratic
path along the valley floor.** You'll find this ride easy and, because of the light traffic, relaxing.

**Bypass the first opportunity to turn right toward Assisi, going
toward Cannara instead.** You'll see Assisi to the right across
the valley like a tiara on the mountain's brow. Stay on this
relatively unremarkable road, made special by its ease. We're
coming in the back door to Assisi.

**Turning up a short rise into the village of Passaggio, turn right
toward Bettona, then right again toward Bastia.** Boulevard-wide
flatness escorts you closer to Assisi. After 3 kilometers you
pass through **Costano**.

**After another 2 kilometers go straight instead of left toward
Bastia.** Don't worry about getting lost at this point, as Assisi
looms in front of you like a beacon. You'll pass under the
SS75 where you'll finally see a sign for Assisi. As you come
into the environs of Assisi be aware that you still have a
3–4-kilometer climb to the pink arches and brilliant symmetry
of the city.

    Assisi is the jewel in the green heart of Umbria. This

city, visible from far, far away, is perched halfway up the slopes of Mt. Subasio. Here, in carefully preserved, austere splendor, is a town which has drawn visitors for hundreds of years. The city is full of art treasures, all of which are easily visited on foot or on your bike. It is a fitting place to end our Umbrian tour for at least two reasons. First, many Umbrians think of Assisi as the best thing they have to offer, and we agree. Second, Assisi is easy to get out of by train. Assisi is about three hours away from Rome or Florence by rail. The station is 5 kilometers out of town in Santa Maria degli Angeli, but it is easy to find by following the Stazione signs from Assisi.

Even if you are not generally moved by cathedrals, it's hard to resist the awesome presence of the basilica of Saint Francis, which is only one of many stunning sights within the walls of the old city. When you feel like resting your eyes from all this sightseeing, step over to the edge of the city walls and feast them on the wide sweep of Umbria that spreads out before you. The tourist information center, which is in the piazza de Commune, will be happy to provide you with a city map and a little write-up on all the major sights in town.

WHERE TO STAY AND DINE IN ASSISI

Our three hotel recommendations are all within the walls of the old city. All are blessed with great views.

The Hotel Subasio (via Frate Elia 2, 06082 Assisi; tel. [075]812206) is probably the fanciest hotel within the city walls. Magnificently furnished in antiques, this former four-teenth-century monastery would be our first recommendation if you are not on a tight budget. It also has the best outside dining terrace in town and is located just down the street from the basilica. (Top)

Our midrange recommendation is the Hotel Posta Panoramic (via San Paolo 17–19, 06081 Assisi; tel. [075]812558), which features a vaulted ceiling dining room and simple but comfortable furnishings. (Medium)

The best bargain in town is the comfortable and quiet Hotel Ristorante Europa, a graceful stone building in a more serene area of the city (via Metastasio 2, 06081 Assisi; tel. [075]816351. (Modest)

All of the hotels we just mentioned have good dining facilities to complement the view.

If you'd like to sit in a restaurant with some real history to it, find Il Medio Evo (via Areo dei Priori 4/b; tel. 813068). The restaurant's foundations date back at least a thousand years. Its hardy cooking equals the massive stonework of the building. There are many pasta dishes available here, and meat eaters may enjoy duck and lamb. Il Medio Evo is closed for part of July. (Medium)

They don't skimp on the truffles at Umbra (vicolo degli Archi 6; tel. 812240). It's near the cathedral and has outdoor seating. (Medium)

If you have been hungering for some authentic Italian garlic bread, the Buca di San Francesco (via Brizi 1; tel. 812204) is the place. *Bruschetta* soaked in olive oil is a favorite here, where a wide range of local cuisine can also be ordered. (Medium)

Assisi has many tiny trattorias and bars where you can get something lighter.

DAILY SUMMARY

UMBRIA TOUR: DAY FIVE

Spoleto to Assisi

(64 kilometers; moderate to challenging)

- Leave Spoleto going down the hill.
- Take the right fork indicating Atre Direzione.
- Go right toward Flaminia.

- Follow the signs toward SS33 and Flaminia, and S. Giacomo at several junctions leading out of town.
- Then take the main road toward Foligno.
- Turn left in San Giacomo after 9 kilometers.
- Follow the sign to Protte.
- In the small village of Protte (unmarked), at the T intersection, go right toward Camporoppolo.
- After less than 1 kilometer, go left toward Camporoppolo.
- Turn right after about 1 kilometer.
- In Bruna, after 3 kilometers, take the left fork—the main road— toward Montefalco.
- At the fork just outside of Bruna, stay left on the main road. (Even though it says Montefalco to the right, we prefer to take this back way, a more scenic route.)
- At the top of the rise, turn right at the small sign to Montefalco, about 2½ kilometers after you began this short climb.
- After 3½ kilometers, turn left toward Montefalco (the sign is a bit faded, or was, so watch for it).
- Follow the signs toward Centro, after 32 kilometers after starting, for lunch in Montefalco.
- After lunch, leave Montefalco toward Foligno.
- Continue right, toward Foligno.
- Six kilometers after descending from Montefalco you'll see a little side road with two signs, Bar Calipso and Panini Vino. Take this road which veers off the main one to the left.
- At the junction 4½ kilometers after you venture into really back roads, turn right over the bridge, then straight toward Bevagna.
- Go left in Bevagna, toward Torre del Colle and Cannara.
- Just outside of the town, take an immediate right toward Cannara.
- Keep following the signs toward Cannara.
- Stay on the main road that bypasses Cantalupo, tracing an erratic path along the valley floor.
- Bypass the first opportunity to turn right toward Assisi, going toward Cannara instead.
- In Passaggio, go right toward Bettona, then right again toward Bastia.
- After another 2 kilometers, go straight instead of left toward Bastia.
- Follow the signs the remaining 4 kilometers into Assisi.

ASSISI

Passaggio

Bevagna

Montefalco

SPOLETO